1977

This book me b

How to Teach Children to
DRAW,
PAINT,
and
USE COLOR

How to Teach Children to DRAW, PAINT, and USE COLOR

Barbara Tuch and Harriet Judy

PARKER PUBLISHING COMPANY, INC.
WEST NYACK, NEW YORK

Library of Congress Cataloging in Publication Data

Tuch, Barbara
    How to teach children to draw, paint, and use color.

    1. Art--Study and teaching (Elementary) I. Judy,
Harriet   joint author. II. Title.
N350.T82   372.5'044   75-8606
ISBN 0-13-435362-5

Printed in the United States of America

This book is dedicated to the creative teachers and children of East Maine School District 63 in Niles, Illinois, who were our inspiration.

A Word from the Authors

Y ou as a teacher are not in a corner by yourself when you wonder, "How can I involve children in an artistic atmosphere when I feel so untalented?" Hundreds of teachers have expressed this feeling to us as Art Coordinators of a large elementary school district. This book can be your guide to developing creativity in yourself, in your children, and in all of your teaching experiences. Gradually you will gain confidence in your own abilities to free your students to think in a new way.

It is not necessary for you to be an expert in painting, drawing or using color to help young people be creative. It *is* necessary, however, for you to have tried each idea, to know what it feels like and to have experienced the possibilities, limitations and pitfalls of each art activity before you motivate someone else. Let us show you how to develop confidence in your ability to teach art.

Once you have experienced the excitement of creating, you can more easily understand how a child feels. You will know why he can't sit still, stay in his seat or worry about the paint that just spilled. He can clean that up later! Just as an artist has his studio, so each child deserves a special place of his own in which to work. Discover how to use the space you have, some available materials and your own ingenuity to create a workshop atmosphere in your classroom.

Each art experience the child has should make him feel that his efforts are worthwhile. His lines or forms or colors are ways of expressing his feelings just as he expresses himself in everyday life. You can learn to recognize, evaluate and encourage self-evaluation in each child's art experience. Few of us will be great artists, but we can try to make art meaningful in our lives.

Many times the very youngster who has been unsuccessful in academic work can achieve in art. If the student is satisfied with his own artistic efforts, the teacher should accept his work at his own level. No marking, grade or teacher's notations or alterations should mar the work.

There are no shortcuts to the development of good taste. It takes years of careful training before a young person realizes that he or she has been growing critically as well as physically and that the selections he or she will make today are not the same as those made last year. When he has learned what to look for, how to recognize skill, craftsmanship, use of media and innovation, the student will confidently apply this knowledge in making decisions or choices in art and in any other subject. Each one will learn to question, "What is well done?" "Which is better?" "If I had to choose, which would it be?"

7

You will learn to encourage the children to incorporate previously learned ideas with new concepts. Once a student has experimented with an art medium, you will be able to draw on interesting ways to encourage him to improve his technique. Then each one will be eager to use materials and techniques innovatively.

You will find this book helpful in many ways. Readers will find practical suggestions for developing an elementary art program. The chapters on methods of using art materials are written with short introductions that precede the discussion of every technique. Then preparation for each lesson is sketched in, while shortcuts and hints are written in detail.

School budgets are tight. No exotic materials are called for in *How to Teach Children to Draw, Paint, and Use Color*. Your school already has most of the materials you will need to build a fine art program. Also, you will learn to make use of scrap materials, part of another idea or to capitalize on a special moment that may never happen again. Through carefully thought-out plans, tricks of the trade and learning how to get, pretrain and use teacher aides, you will find that teaching art is fun.

The environment you and the children live in at school will change as you learn new ways to display children's work and inspire them with provocative exhibits. You will develop ways to encourage creative expression, individual interpretation and idea experimentation without fear of failure.

Many books on teaching art present isolated projects. *How to Teach Children to Draw, Paint, and Use Color* will equip you to organize a comprehensive art program that builds on skills. Resources and motivational material are listed separately for easy reference. You will be introduced to new ideas and products so that you can decide which will work for you. Then, too, you will learn how to get help when you need it, find out how to have a constant source of ideas and gain skill in developing a new idea further.

Just as a successful art program is the building up of experiences, this book is written as a series of related activities. Once a student has worked with an art skill, you, the teacher, will be able to draw on interesting ways to encourage him to improve his technique. This book is designed so you can leaf through it the first time and then use it specifically as a cross-reference. As you reread it, you will begin to develop a sensitivity and find yourself recognizing opportunities to bring art experiences into your daily curriculum.

Art is not a handicraft; it is the transmission of
feeling the artist has experienced. (Tolstoy)

Barbara Tuch and Harriet Judy

Acknowledgments

We appreciate the help of Livia Hyman Klein, Donna Meilach, Lin Kempin, David J. Judy, Detlef Koska, William Pineless, Ralph, Kerri and Andy Tuch, and George, Claudia and Jane Judy, who all shared their talents with us.

Contents

CONTENTS

CONTENTS

14

1 The Workshop Atmosphere—
I Know Where I'm Going:
Planning an Art Lesson

Your art program should be a sequential one that builds on skills from year to year.

THE FIRST STEP
THROW OUT
patterns
preconceived notions

Since this book deals only with drawing, painting and using color, we will not explain a total art curriculum. Your school district will probably have an art guide or you can send for one from your state office of public instruction. In this chapter we will present some ways for you to teach any kind of art lesson in your program using the workshop atmosphere.

There is no reason a lesson in art should be more trouble than any other. Realize how few art lessons you have taught compared with math, language arts, social studies and science, which you teach almost every day.

Art has many experiences in common with other subjects.

LET THE CHILD
experiment and explore
be innovative
work on his or her own level

take a project one step further whenever he can
learn from his peers
have sufficient time to set up and clean up

All of us become bogged down in routine, sometimes get snarled in confusion or into a rut in our teaching and planning. Often we lose the significance of an art lesson.

LET AN ART LESSON GROW OUT OF
a surprising turn of events
a language arts lesson
a math or science session
a new thought

Dr. Ray V. Stapp, Professor of Art at Eastern Illinois University in Charleston, Illinois, suggests guidelines to help you evaluate each art lesson you present.*

Select your lesson and try to have it fit as many of the following criteria as possible.

Is there a learning experience in the lesson?
Does the project challenge the children at their level?
Is there an opportunity for more than one solution?
Can children make decisions and judgments for themselves?
Is there an opportunity for each child to express his own ideas or feelings in an original, creative way?
Can the child choose and use materials innovatively in his own way?
Will the child be able to combine this skill with other ideas to express himself?
Does this lesson come as a natural outgrowth of a previous one and provide opportunities for another lesson to follow naturally?

In addition, an art lesson should *contribute to the total esthetic growth of the child*.

You wouldn't think of teaching an academic lesson without preparation. Art lessons must likewise have goals and teach the skills necessary to reach them.

Motivation is needed to stimulate interest. However, *beware of slick examples*. These encourage mere copying. Spend time before all presentations getting your class into a receptive, enthusiastic attitude.

Try the lesson in advance yourself. When you've had the fun of creating, you will know how the child feels.

Art skills are just as important as any other part of the curriculum. Teach each art lesson with a purpose, not just to fill time.

Avoid tricky, gimmicky projects that do not meet a child's developmental needs or involve creative action on his part. Art is not something to do when there is nothing else to do. Creativity cannot be developed in one or two hours of art a week. Encourage creative thinking all day long.

Arts and Activities, May, 1967.

The Workshop Atmosphere

Developing Creative Action

Does your classroom have a workshop atmosphere? The room arrangement should be flexible enough to allow for many kinds of activities. Sometimes the center of the room should be cleared for working on the floor. Other times groups of desks and chairs might be needed.

Creative action follows an interest. Find a spot in the room to display art books, magazines and current events happening in the arts.

A creative environment will provide and encourage

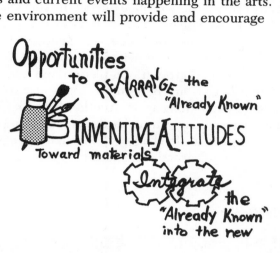

Opportunities to REARRANGE the "Already Known"

INVENTIVE ATTITUDES Toward materials

Integrate the "Already Known" into the new

From Your Freedom to Their Security

When were you last inspired? Are you eager to learn new skills? Do you have a receptive attitude toward innovative methods? Are you willing to make a mistake as you learn? Permit yourself these freedoms. Children are observant and will feel more confident if you do.

An expert feels secure. How does anyone become an expert? Obviously it takes time, practice, patience and that extra something. Do we as teachers really permit a child to become a specialist? So many teachers feel that if they have done painting or stitchery or any other art lesson once during the semester they must go on to something else. Help children discover how a skill can really be used. This time use one previously learned technique combined with another. For instance, if the class knows how to paint with watercolor without additional instruction, let the children use watercolor for the background of a picture and add markers or ink to supply the details. In this way they are building on skills and still do not have the feeling that they are doing the same thing again. Another time they may decide to use construction paper shapes pasted on a watercolor design. By using materials again in different ways art skills are expanded. In chapters 3 through 8 you will find numerous suggestions on how to use newly learned skills in other ways.

Now I Know Myself:
Encouraging Self-Evaluation

If each child's work is accepted honestly, he will develop confidence in himself. He will be willing to accept evaluation and realize that sometimes one's work is more successful than at other times.

How many youngsters in your group are self-motivated enough to correct their own errors without being asked to? These are the children who are trying to excel. Let them. They may not need your help at this time. Work with those who need encouragement.

The Workshop Atmosphere

Avoid praising too highly or insincerely. Yes, there are some children in whose work there is really little to compliment. Look for something, even if it is small, where you can truthfully say, "You have done a good job." But, if a child has the feeling that he has not done his best, respect his opinion. Overpraise may accomplish the opposite of what you intend and can actually hamper creativity. We've heard the story of the adult who still can only draw the same horse picture he made in the first grade; he did it so well then and was praised so highly that he has been afraid ever since to show that he knows how to make anything else.

When the student has a reason to learn, he will solve many problems himself and ask for help only when needed.

If a child uses art media freely, easily and with conviction, has new tools to use, likes to experiment and create new ways of working, then his learning has been successful.

You will have created a workshop atmosphere if you build on previous skills, encourage experimentation and permit mistakes in a room that allows for freedom of movement and thought.

2 Make Things Easy from Beginning to End: A New Beginning for You

Each September let a new creative "you" emerge. Start with confidence. Throw out those old-fashioned trace-around patterns and holiday-centered projects. Instead plan an art skills program for the entire school year.

No program should be rigid. Your class will differ in abilities and personality from year to year so adjust your art program to fit it. In an area where the children are weak or inexperienced plan several lessons developing the new art skill you have introduced in a prior lesson. Don't go too fast. Remember no one knits a sweater during his first knitting lesson.

You may find that your group does extremely well in a certain art skill. Give them many opportunities to work in that area so they will excel.

If you have a love of a particular medium, your enthusiasm could be the inspiration for many lessons. Once the boys and girls know how to use an art material or technique, let them experiment.

Think of how many drawings and paintings an artist does in one medium in a lifetime. Don't be afraid to repeat and expand upon a good lesson. Try it again in a new way. Use your imagination and let the children use theirs.

The following list suggests drawing, painting and color materials that should be introduced in kindergarten and be embroidered upon in each succeeding grade level. Do not assume that all the pupils are proficient in each skill. Give them opportunities to show what they can do. Then plan your lessons to accommodate their needs.

Drawing with	Painting with	Using Color
Sticks	Water	Construction Paper
Brushes	Finger Paint	Tissue
Markers	Watercolor	Crayons
Charcoal	Powder Paint	Dye
Crayon	Tempera	Stain
Chalk	Tempera Cakes	Collage
Pencils	Acrylics	Weaving
	Markers	Stitchery
		Calligraphy
		Rubbings

Prevent Problems Before They Occur

As art coordinators working with hundreds of teachers each year, we have encountered many questions and problems that may be similar to yours. These may sound familiar:

Can You Be Sure It Works?

It is imperative that you try a lesson first. Then you will know the pitfalls, the possibilities and the level of difficulty before you present it to your group.

How Do You Start an Art Lesson?

Take the time to introduce the lesson clearly. Be sure to allow enough time. Sometimes several sessions are needed to complete the work. State the objectives and explain what is expected. Briefly tell the rules or limitations. Have all the supplies out and ready to use. Be enthusiastic and ready to help when it is necessary. Vary the motivation; a demonstration, movies, a guest artist, photographs, a story, record or several samples are all good to use. Try not to use the same motivation for every art session.

What Is the Best Way to End a Lesson?

Let the class know how long they will work. Ten minutes before cleanup remind the children to start finishing their work or prepare to put it away for another time. Cover the paint, paste or glue. Put away the extra supplies. Have some children help collect brushes while others are preparing a display.

What If There Never Is Time to Finish Anything?

Perhaps you are planning too much for one session. Was the motivation too long? Is it possible to allow time for longer art periods? Did you have supplies and tools out before the lesson?

What Can I Do for a Quickie Art Project?

Don't have one. A hurry-up art lesson is like trying to catch a plane flight at the last minute. You might catch it, or you might not. Do something else.

Make Things Easy from Beginning to End

What Can We Make for Thanksgiving,
Easter, Christmas?

Plan a sequential art program stressing skills, not projects. To provide the child with a good art background, he must slowly acquire good taste. Most holiday projects are classic examples of garish or poor taste. In many classes entirely too much time is spent on holiday art, which neither the parent nor the child can use once the special day is over.

An original picture, letter or card accompanied by a well-designed wall decoration, piece of pottery or sculpture, or a hand-designed and sewn item using a previously learned skill will encourage holiday spirit and enrich your art program at the same time.

How Can Copying Be Discouraged?

Let the class know you want each pupil to experiment and see how original he can be. Don't praise a child publicly while the others are still working. Wait until evaluation time. You can always encourage a youngster by quietly speaking to him at his desk.

What If We Run Out of Time
Because of an Emergency Situation?

Give short, simple instructions. Paints can be covered with plastic wrap or foil and set on a worktable for another day. Disposable and replaceable items can be discarded. Use small quantities of glue and paint to begin with. They are easier to refill than pour back. Assign each child a cleanup job as it is needed. Use buckets as well as sinks for cleanup. Train each class member at the start of the school year where things go and what the cleanup procedure is.

Can Wastefulness Be Discouraged?

Set a good example. Use the proper tool for each job. Know which paper is best used for the project. Choose small paper for a small job. Spell out how materials are to be used and in what quantity. Encourage correcting one's own work or working on the reverse side rather than discarding paper. Teach how to erase, paint or paste over and use scraps effectively.

Is It Possible to Have a Quiet Art Lesson?

Not all the time. Some lessons require banging, movements or discussions. Most children are animated. However, there are many art activities where each student is totally engrossed, such as crayon etching, detailed construction or collage, watercolor painting, sketching, observing through a magnifying glass and drawing.

What If I Run Out of Ideas?

You won't if you have an art program built on skills rather than projects. Have confidence in yourself. Use a previously learned skill and add a new one. Stretch your imagination. Keep an art file and use source material in books and art magazines. Avoid copying and isolated gimmicky projects.

An Easy Cleanup
Using Disposable Materials

Once your students know that there is a use for odds and ends from the kitchen, you will have a constant supply with just a little encouragement. Recycling clean, empty containers of all sorts is an easy and inexpensive way to get art supplies. Some things can be reused many times and others are just used for one lesson and discarded. This will simplify cleanup.

Start with:
    Two wastebaskets—one for disposable, burnable materials and one for
        aerosol cans and nonburnables

Add:
    Newspapers to cover desks and floor
    Egg cartons as paint containers or to hold small items like buttons, tacks and
        nails
    Plastic container lids to hold glue, small amounts of paint or as palettes
    Gallon milk cartons, washed out and cut down
    Styrofoam meat trays
    Juice cans for water or paint

    Baby food jars or other small jars with screw tops
    Coffee cans for dye, sand, wax, markers, etc.
    Plastic bleach-type bottles as pitchers for the painting lessons
Don't forget:
    Sticks for mixing
    Margarine-type tubs with covers and storage containers
    Small cartons for scrap collections and yarn
    Plastic bags and ties for damp or very dirty items

Make Things Easy from Beginning to End

And:

> Hand soap, scraps or free small bars of soap (hotel bar soap) rarely provided
> by schools but often needed
> Paper towels
> Sponges
> Rags

Avoid using partitioned metal or plastic paint palettes or anything else that takes scrubbing and extra time to clean up at the end of a busy lesson. Make things easy for yourself. Teach the students to clean up after themselves. With disposable materials nothing could be easier.

Room Arrangements and Places to Work

I just don't have room for an art corner! Are you sure? With thought, planning and rearranging what you have, it is possible to find a place in your room for an art corner and a storage place for easily available art materials.

Let's think of a way to set up an art corner first. Try to arrange the art lessons and storage area near a sink. A large table and chairs are nice to have, as well as a few double-faced painting easels. The total amount of space need not be great. If you are lucky enough to have room for a few children to work at a table or at the easels in the art corner, this is fine. If your space is small, create a spot where the children can go for materials to use.

The back of a piano, filing cabinets, or a bookcase can be used as a room divider for the art corner. Nail some cork panels on the back and sides of the cabinets you use as the divider or glue them on metal furniture. The cork forms a bulletin board to display the creative work.

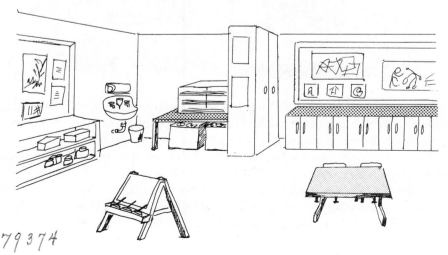

79374

Now, organize your materials creatively. Get some big, sturdy, cardboard boxes, oatmeal boxes, large tubes (gift wrap often comes on 3″ wide cardboard tubes), large coffee cans with lids, divided boxes and large thin ones that can hold assorted sizes of art paper. Look around and be a saver. A good, strong carton designed to ship items safely is often an indispensable storage container for you. Begin making some storage modules. With the art materials you want to use in mind, cut the boxes to hold paper, brushes, chalk, crayons, and so on. Clay can be kept in plastic bags inside cans or preferably large plastic containers with lids. Brushes will be stored, as suggested in chapter 6, in large coffee cans.

When your storage module is glued and constructed, cover it with attractive plastic adhesive paper or paint it with bright, waterproof paint. Your time and effort will be well spent because these storage units are quite durable.

Extra-large boxes can be kept under a table or sink to hold scrap materials (Styrofoam, wood, egg cartons, etc.) for constructions.

Another big box can hold scraps of many kinds of paper. This can include odd pieces of construction paper, as well as foil, cellophane, used gift wrap or tissue, and other paper treasures. Cover or paint these boxes, too.

Make Things Easy from Beginning to End

On top of the table you can keep an assortment of many kinds of art paper. Separate them by size and kind by cutting away one end of the boxes, glue them together and finish the outside. The boxes must be of one size. The children will enjoy taking their papers from the filing containers.

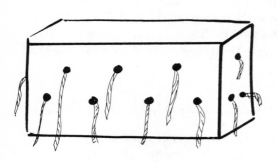 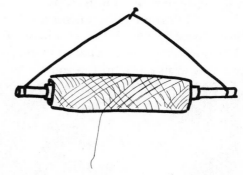

A Yarn Box—Wrap yarn in balls. Punch holes in a large, covered box, pull the ends of the yarn through the holes. Each child can cut off as much yarn as needed and the yarn will not tangle. String can be put on a dowel rod for easy access.

A Secret Idea Box—It is fun to keep a "secret box" in the art corner. On small slips of paper write some ideas for pictures to draw or paint, a construction project, or a clay subject. Cut a hole in the top so the children can reach in for an idea. The papers can be put back for others to use, because artists interpret ideas in many ways. This box helps a young artist who can't think of anything to do.

If you have plenty of cupboards, shelves and bookcases available, use these wisely and you won't have to make your own storage containers. Put materials where the children can reach them. Put your things up high. Shelves can usually be moved in a storage unit to accommodate different-sized objects. Don't forget to use the sides and doors for displaying art.

How to Use the Art Corner

Establish some rules that the whole class clearly understands:

>   What do we use to protect the work area?
>   When can we use the art corner?
>   Where can we work?

Who cleans up?
What do we do with our art work?

It is best to keep about three or four media ready to use and change them frequently so the children always have something new and challenging to work with.

Children can be encouraged to display their own work on the cork bulletin board areas or take it home, whichever pleases them. The teacher can make a large class portfolio from cardboard to keep drawings. Then there will always be plenty of pictures to use around the room.

Where to Work Outside the Art Center

If your art corner is small and is used only as a materials center, allow those whose work is finished to select their supplies and return to their own table or desk to work.

When they are finished they return their supplies, display their work or dry it and clean up.

Drying Areas

Windowsills, tops of tables, or under tables are good drying areas. Keep plenty of newspaper available to put down under each work. A folding clothes rack makes a good place to dry pictures. In addition to the wooden rods on the rack, add some plastic clotheslines of your own. Tie a bag of clip clothespins at the side of the rack and let the children hang their pictures there until dry. Commercially made metal racks are available for drying art work, but they are expensive.

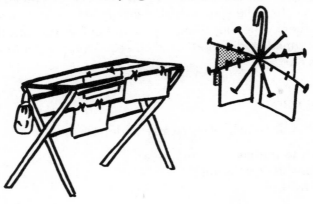

Make Things Easy from Beginning to End

The Outdoors as a Place to Work

When the weather permits, the outdoors is the best place in the world for art. Large mural paper can be taped on walls or fences and each artist is given a place to work. Don't do this on a windy day.

Sketch pads can be made if you save cardboard tablet backs. Tape, staple or use metal clips or clip clothespins to hold paper on the pad. Small drawstring bags are nice to hold pencils, crayons, charcoal or chalk. This can be worn on the wrist as the child sketches. His materials will be handy and not easily lost. Chapter 5 has more ideas for outdoor drawing and painting.

Some good outdoor projects, in addition to drawing and painting, are tie-dyeing, modeling with Sculptamold or gray clay. Pariscraft work is best when done outdoors because the plaster dust blows away. Constructing with wood, glue and nails is much quieter outdoors. Macramé work can be tied to a fence. Weaving can be done with a stick tied to a fence. Warp threads are added to the stick and another strong branch or rod is woven into the bottom warp. Tie the ends of the warp together and begin weaving.

Cooperation

Everyone must cooperate if art is to be a pleasure. You and the children should plan cleanup—whether you have a committee or each child cleans up for himself is up to those involved, but duties must be clearly understood.

Preparation

In preparing an art lesson, an art corner or a large group project, you must prepare everything in advance. Children enjoy helping you pass out paper, pour paint into containers, put water on tables, distribute brushes and many other jobs. Make sure each child has a job he enjoys and can do successfully and quickly.

Large group projects will be more successful if you've planned ahead and are prepared. Selection of groups and leaders is important and each participant should know his duties.

Pretrain Assistants and Teacher Aides

A great help to a teacher is a group of pretrained teacher aides. The older children in the school or competent children in your class can be used for this as well as mothers, fathers, volunteers or paid aides. Be sure these people know the lesson, know the skills involved as well as you do, have met before the lesson and planned their role in the lesson and cleanup. They can free you to work with children who require more attention than others.

3   A Line Can Do Anything

Have you ever noticed what children draw on scraps of paper, on the covers of their notebooks, or in the margins of dittoed material? A great variety of marvelous line drawings often appear. In these doodles you will find exciting use of line indicating the children's interests and reflections of how they feel about themselves and others. Why do some children do tiny, detailed work while others scribble, use bold lines or draw geometric abstracts?

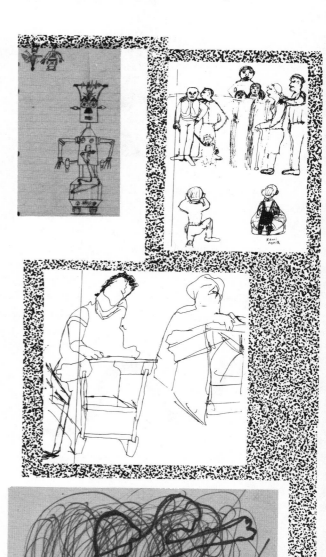

Drawing is personal. Each child will develop a unique drawing style much like an individual handwriting style. To help children appreciate this, show them line drawings by famous artists, from Michelangelo and Da Vinci to Toulouse-Lautrec, Picasso, Wyeth and Matisse. They will see that all artists have a distinctive way of drawing and using line. Discourage copying current popular cartoons or commercial symbols, which they love to imitate.

Drawing is so important that children should have many experiences to develop free and inventive use of lines. Have them create with many media such as pencil, charcoal, marker, string, sticks, crayon, chalk and brush. Provide enough opportunity to draw in the art program so that children will not become self-conscious about drawing as they grow older.

A Line Can Do Anything

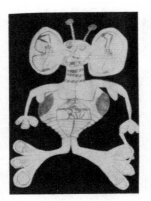

"I can't draw a straight line" is a typical remark we hear from adults. Why should we draw a straight line when there are so many more creative lines that we can draw freely and with conviction? Let's help children loosen up their drawings as we explore the variety of line.

I Am Free:
Loosening Up with Lines

Help your class have fun with lines by playing a game with them. Ask them this question—"What is a line?" Write the question on the board. They will have some difficulty in answering your question. Let them come up to the board and draw what they are trying to say. Usually they begin with a straight line.

"Who has another kind of line to show us? Come and whisper its name to me. Then draw it and see if the class can guess what kind of line you know."

Thick lines   Thin lines

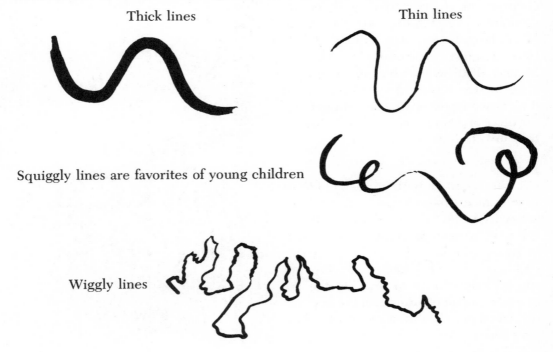

Squiggly lines are favorites of young children

Wiggly lines

A Line Can Do Anything

Zigzag lines

Curved

You might guide them at this point with this line.
"What is it? A tall line!"

Other lines

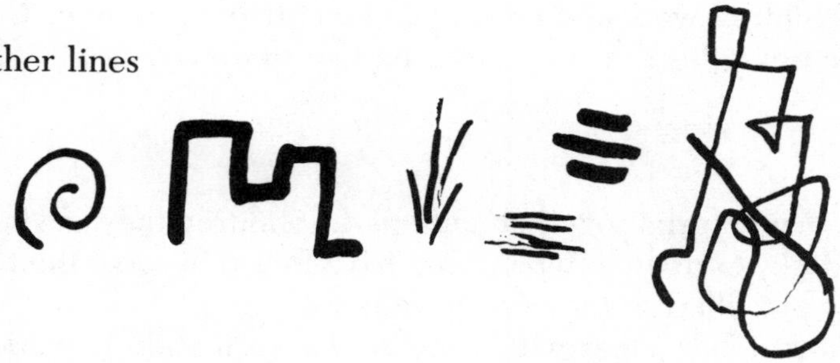

Overlapping lines 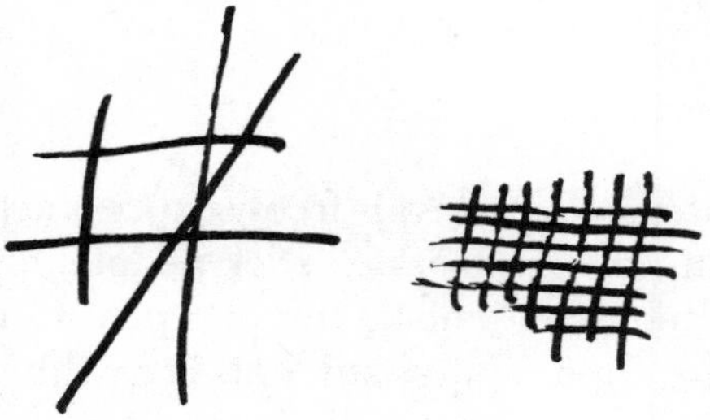    Broken lines

Now and then you can draw a line to lead them in a new direction. After the game the children will realize that there are many kinds of lines to use in their drawings. Erase the examples when the game is ended.

Getting Ready

> Pencils (primary are best) or charcoal
> Newsprint (2 pieces)

Let's Begin

"On your first piece of paper draw as many lines as you can remember from our game, or invent some new ones. Everyone should have at least seven different lines but do as many as you can. Don't forget to make some thick and some thin, or some tall ones. I will give you ten minutes to do this. Look at your lines. What do some of them remind you of? On your second piece of paper draw a line picture that uses many kinds of lines." Suggest some topics as "Getting Lost in a Crowd" or "Packing My Suitcase" or "Wandering in the Forest."

How Did It Work?
(Keep this evaluation personal)

Walk around as the children work and encourage inventive use of line. Help the child think of ways to improve his drawing. Does he like to draw?

What Else?

Staple several pieces of newsprint together and tell the children they can keep these sketchbooks in their desks to draw in when they have free time. Ask them to give them to you when they are filled so they can have more paper.

Put up large pieces of butcher paper with a section for each child to work in during a rainy day recess.

Draw on the board. Be sure the children know this must be erased and only done when they have permission.

Figures in Action

Children in kindergarten through the intermediate levels freely express action figures in art but by the upper grades they often revert to "safe" stick people. They are no longer willing to take a chance that someone may make fun of a picture of a person who doesn't look like one. Luckily, in the upper grades students are willing to try something new. It is a good idea to try art lessons that will renew their confidence. Plan several sessions on figure drawing, each with a different approach. Three excellent ones are shadow figures, quick marker drawings and overlapping figures. Try these as a unit.

A Line Can Do Anything

Getting Ready

> Long-handled ½" easel brushes
> 1" of black tempera in individual orange juice cans
> 3 sheets of 12" x 18" paper for each child clipped to a piece of cardboard used as a drawing board
> One person (at a time) to pose as model
> Cleanup rags
> Simple props (a chair, wastepaper basket, box or the like)
> One 5' string with a rock attached at one end

Let's Begin

"How do people move?" "What parts of the body can bend?" "What is under the skin that helps us move?" "Why do we sometimes fall?" "What is balance?"

After a short discussion of muscles and bones, take the string and hold it next to a model who is standing with his feet a few inches apart. The string is held directly in front of him starting at his forehead as the rock hangs down and nearly reaches the floor. "We will pretend that this balance line goes straight through the person. He is standing symmetrically and his body is steady. What would happen if his legs were suddenly pulled forward?" Demonstrate this by putting a chair under him (after he has been warned). "He would lose his balance and fall if nothing were there for him to lean on."

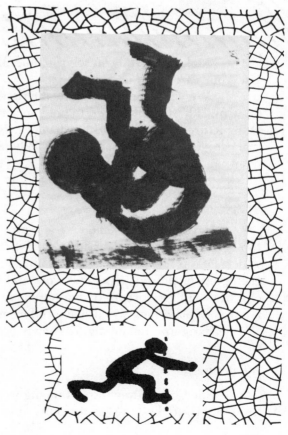

"Can someone balance on one foot? Yes, if one foot is under the head." Show this with string. "Of course, your own balance line is really invisible."

35

"Now we will paint people in many different positions using our brushes and the black tempera. We aren't interested in what someone is wearing or if he or she wears glasses or has long or short hair. The important thing is to show what the person is doing. Is he running, has he fallen, is he holding something heavy, is he playing tennis, jumping rope or pushing something? What part of his body is bent? What part is straight? Where would the balance line be if it were visible? If the model is leaning over, make him really lean. How could we show he is pushing hard?

"Make sure you can see the model. If you can't, quietly move someplace else. Use your cardboard as a desk.

"We will have one person at a time model in the pose I suggest. We'll have to draw quickly since it is hard to hold an action position for more than a minute or two. Our pictures should look like shadows. No detail, just the action. Work as large as you can. Use broad brush strokes. When you have used one paper, flip it over and paint on the one underneath."

How Did It Work?

Have each pupil choose the figure drawing he considers his best and put it on top of the others. Display the piles of pictures on the floor. See if the others can tell which actions are shown. Which really look like they are doing something? Next have each person choose his poorest work and tell why he feels it wasn't successful. Many children will be surprised that someone else is pleased with what he considers a failure. Explain how we all have different opinions, all of which have value.

Hang up as many figure drawings as possible, overlapping them if necessary.

What Else?

Encourage drawing action figures with markers in a second lesson. Each drawing is to be one continuous line made without lifting the marker from

A Line Can Do Anything

the paper. The student works as quickly as he can again using the model for inspiration. To emphasize the action, or to correct the drawing, lines are overlapped. Exaggeration, rather than realism, is stressed. "What is the model doing?" "How is his body bent? Make it look even more bent."

For a third lesson, several different figures should be drawn on one piece of paper using a different color marker each time. The paper can be turned sideways or upside down to give an all-over effect. Be sure to vary the pose of each model. One can be stretching, one might have fallen down, another can sit, etc.

Any time in the future, when a student is drawing figures, remind him to get a friend to model for him.

Movement—Animals

A Line Can Do Anything

Children have an empathy for animals. Many have pets, most have been to the zoo and all have seen T.V. specials about them. Young children willingly pretend to be animals and will pantomime crawling, jumping, running and hopping movements without hesitation. Take advantage of this eagerness to teach a lesson in animal movement.

Getting Ready

Soft charcoal or primary pencils—no erasers
12″ x 18″ manila paper—each child should have several pieces on his desk in a
    pile

Let's Begin

"How does a cat look when he's sleeping? Tell me how a horse's legs look when he jumps over a fence. How can a giraffe reach so high? Did you ever see a mother animal look over her shoulder to see if the baby is still behind?

"Hold your pencil lightly. Use lines that overlap and see if you can get some of them to look dark and others light. Make some thick and some thin. Listen to what I say and draw as I talk.

"Tiny kittens are asleep all rolled up so close to each other we can hardly see the end of the one and the beginning of another. Their fur is soft and fuzzy. One looks up, turns her head and yawns. Another fluffy creature climbs over the rest.

"Take another piece of paper. What happens when we stretch? We look longer and thinner. Let's show that. We will exaggerate. Really show stretching.

"Take another paper. Pretend we're all at the zoo. The giraffes are outside eating leaves from the tree. A little one can't quite reach and stretches as high as he can but can only reach the lower branches. The mother animal has something in her mouth and bends over to give it to the baby."

A Line Can Do Anything

You, the teacher, can tell or read other simple but descriptive paragraphs about animals doing things familiar to the children. Talk about groups of the same kind of animal for the first few lessons. Stress movement rather than accuracy.

How Did It Work?

"Who has tried something new? Find the pictures that really show movement and action. Which drawing shows a specific action? Has anyone made good use of exaggeration?"

What Else?

Try the same lesson using watercolors or crayon. Encourage freedom of line, fast lines, slow ones and those that show expression.

Machines

All children are potential inventors. Each child should be encouraged to plan, correct his plans and then finalize them. Snap judgments are easy to make but are they always best? Drawing blueprints and constructing imaginary or real machines are fun but take preplanning and reasoning skills. Allow enough time for this lesson. One art lesson can be used to sort out materials from the scrap box and carefully take large pieces or complicated mechanisms apart. Another day work on plans and corrections and only then begin the actual construction.

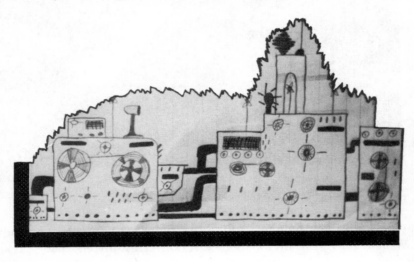

Getting Ready

Samples of blueprints and sketches of inventions for the children to look at, i.e.: DaVinci, Bell, Edison, Fulton

Old, dismantled watches, motors, gears, beads, springs, game parts, wheels, spools, etc.

Wood scraps

Scissors

Glue

Colored construction paper

Cardboard

String, wire

Toothpicks

Soft, nonhardening clay

Blocks of Styrofoam packing pieces

Fabric scraps

Pencils, markers

Nails, hammers, wire clippers

A Line Can Do Anything

Let's Begin

"What good would a machine be if it didn't do anything? Who thinks up all the ideas? What are inventions?

"We are going to be inventors today. You can work alone or with one or two others. First think of something that is hard to do, or of a job that you don't like to do. Now invent a way to make it easier. Use pencil lines to show how your machine will work. Make a picture or diagram first to show your plans.

"In science we've talked about gears, inclined planes, wheels and pulleys. Include some of these simple machines in your invention. Yesterday we took all the mechanical objects apart so just take what you or your group will need. Decide how your invention will work and what it will do. Sometimes a piece of cardboard, Styrofoam or wood can be used as a base or as an important part of your invention. Be sure to try many arrangements to see which is best. See how the pieces fit together. If something doesn't look right, change it. Turn it around, use it in a different way, or put it back and choose something else. If you can't find the right part, make it. Use string or wire to connect your pieces. Clay can hold some parts together, too.

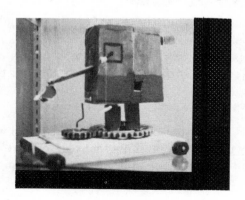

"Your line diagram can help explain your invention. First use light pencil lines and after you have made your corrections, use markers. Inventors try to improve their plans. Your machine doesn't actually have to work but it should look as if it could. Be prepared to explain how it should move. Have a list of parts you have used.

"Display your invention along with the diagram you made on the tables or windowsills."

How Did It Work?

How are the lines used in our machines?
Do the inventions look like machines?
Do they look as if they could function?
Do the parts look connected?
Do the diagrams help to explain the machines?
Which would you like to buy if it really did work?

What Else?

Make a booklet using diagrams of inventions that belong together.

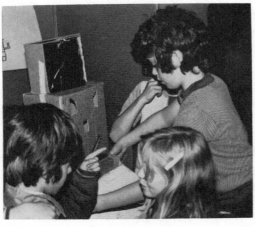

See if the boys and girls are able to follow the directions to make someone else's machine. Have the inventor supervise.

For a less mature group have the children make their machines two-dimensional rather than three-dimensional. Boys and girls might draw first and then use fabric or wallpaper and work the inventions out as collages, or use wood or cardboard. Make sure string or lines are used to connect the parts.

It's Fun to Do Abstract Drawing

"I can't draw!" How often have you heard this and wished you could give the child enough security to create something that pleases him? Abstraction allows one to draw the necessary lines and shape of an object and arrange them in a new way.

A Line Can Do Anything

With the class study the work of cubists Georges Braque and Picasso. See how they drew and discuss how the children can see new ways to draw their own subject. There are several ways to develop abstraction with young children.

Getting Ready

Pencil or marker or black crayon
12″ x 18″ manila paper for each child

Let's Begin

"Let's fold our paper in half and in half again so that we have four small areas. Today I want you to draw anything that is in your desk that you can take out and look at later. Glue bottles, books, scissors, crayons, pencils, are all good things to draw. Put this into the first box on your paper.

"After we have drawn from memory, take out the *same* object you drew in the first box and carefully draw what you see in the second box. Is the first or the second a more detailed drawing? Did you forget some parts in your first picture? In the third box let's pretend we can take apart the object you drew and arrange these shapes separately. Don't forget important spaces where there is nothing, like the holes in the handle of your scissors.

"Now in the last box let's rearrange all the parts in a new way. You may repeat shapes, lines and textures—use *only* the shapes in the third box. Now we have taken an object and used its shapes and lines in a new way. This is abstraction."

How Did It Work?

"What have you learned? Can we draw more accurately from memory or by seeing? Are both good ways to draw? Could you abstract some other things? Who has used the lines and shapes most creatively?"

What Else?

Draw portraits then abstract them.

Have children draw secret objects in an abstract manner.

Young children:

Draw a shape on a 4" x 4" piece of paper. Cut it out.

Trace it on a 9" x 12" manila paper. Overlap it and turn it again and again until the entire area is covered. Let the shape go off the paper at the edges. Now take crayons and color or design the *new* shapes created by the overlapping. By arranging our shape in a new way we have created an abstract design in which the original shape is not recognizable.

A Line Can Do Anything

Drawing and Seeing*

All of us look, but what do we see? How much do we miss?

Getting Ready

9″ x 12″ construction paper, mixed colors
12″ x 18″ manila paper
Sharpened pencils
Tripod magnifying glasses (one for each child)
Dried weeds and seeds

Let's Begin

The children enter the art room but the teacher remains in the background. On each table, arranged in an abstract manner, are pieces of construction paper, each slightly overlapping another.

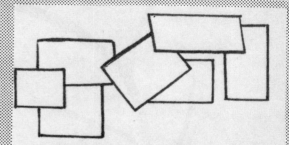

On every rectangle there is one of several varieties of dried flower stems or pods. A sign reads: "What do you see? Look carefully." The youngsters handle the dried objects, some examine them thoughtfully while others look hastily. The art teacher mills among the children encouraging careful observation. Each youngster is asked to take a piece of construction paper and a dried flower or stem to his seat.

"Today we're going to do an experiment. We want to find out how observant we are—how well do we really see? Artists and scientists have trained themselves to see things that others miss. We are going to train ourselves to do the same thing."

Small tripod magnifying glasses are distributed. Many of the children don't recognize what they are holding. A short discussion brings out that these are dried flower pods and stems. Poppy and milkweed cases, cattails, stems with thorns, Queen Anne's lace, delphinium, peony leaves and columbine are a good variety to begin with.

Each one looks closely, turns his flower in different directions and uses the magnifying glass. He may decide to hold the dried plant near the colored paper for contrast.

The children are encouraged to verbalize what they see as the teacher walks around. "Are you sure? What shape is the stem? Would it roll? At what angle would the leaves come from it?" are questions asked.

The drawing paper and pencils are ready to use. The children have noticed that the magnifying glass enlarges what they have seen with their eyes. As artists often exaggerate form and shape, in this lesson *size* is exaggerated.

*From "What Do You See," Barbara Tuch, *Arts and Activities*, Jan. 1971, pp. 22-23. Used by permission of the publisher.

"With our eyes we'll exaggerate the size of our dried plants even more than the magnifying glass has done. Use a pencil to show what your object really looks like. Draw the shape and details exactly as you have observed. Make sure you've looked at your plant from all angles. Draw as large as you can and put in as many details as you see. Take your time. Let your drawing go off the page. See if you can show how the stem curves, twists and turns. Are there some parts that are flat, broken off or hollow? Show that."

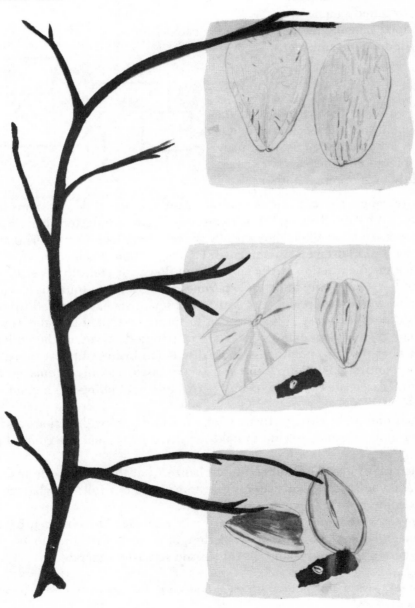

A Line Can Do Anything

This may be the quietest art lesson you've taught. The children are totally absorbed. Those who are more adept will draw in great detail, but those who are not as confident will have good results, too. For the older children or those who are more mature, questions of shading and perspective can be answered. Drawings of several stems or seed pods may be illustrated on one paper.

Children's comments like "Look at the holes here" or "Each seed is really a different shape" reflect discoveries that fascinate each observer.

How Did It Work?

The children can arrange a class exhibit of the drawings. Let them compare what they have seen.

How well have they observed? Have they shown things that were not easily visible to the casual viewer?

What Else?

Follow-up lessons on design can be planned. By using these drawings, or better still, the actual dried plants, the children quickly find interesting shapes that can be exaggerated or repeated for good designs. Color can be introduced at this point. Linoleum block designs or tissue collages are further paths to explore.

For a future reference lesson or a jumping-off point, "Drawing and Seeing" is indispensable.

Contour Drawing

"Have you ever tried to draw an object by drawing the outer edges of what you see without looking at your drawing? It is fun and surprising to see how your hand can interpret what your eye is seeing. Contour drawing has a special look. There will be distortion, particularly at first. The lines will be clear and bold, not fuzzy like a sketch line.

"When doing a contour drawing, keep your wrist stiff and let your hand move rather than the fingers.

"Try to complete the drawing without looking at the paper, but if it is absolutely necessary, look at your paper for a second to check the results."

Older children enjoy the freedom of contour drawing and like the special look. It helps them overcome self-consciousness about drawing.

Getting Ready

Movie—*Contour Drawing*
Drawings of Henri Matisse and Ben Shahn
Opaque projector and screen
Drawing tools—pencils or markers
Lots of newsprint
Objects to draw—easy shapes at first—from kindergarten, wooden toys; music room, instruments; large cans, bottles, wooden blocks; objects in the desk, crayons, glue, pencils; objects in the classroom, clock, desk, book, chair.

Let's Begin

"We have seen the movie about contour drawing. Now let's look at some drawings of Henri Matisse or Ben Shahn. Both were expert at contour drawing and choosing only parts that were important to draw. Today we will try some contour drawing of our own. Remember: We draw as we look at the object and our hand moves on the paper moving no faster than our eyes. Work slowly and carefully. Really observe. I will walk among you because I want to be sure you are really contour drawing and are trusting your eyes and hand. You will want to do many drawings to master this new way of working. This is not any more difficult to do, after some practice, than bouncing a basketball while keeping your eyes on the basket."

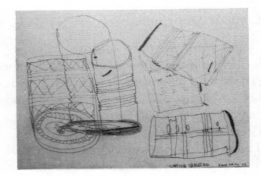

How Did It Work?

"Did you enjoy contour drawing? Can you see the special look in our pictures? Have you learned to trust your hand more as you draw?"

What Else?

This is a good lesson to use more than one time. Go from objects to hands and faces of classmates. Then allow children to pose and have the class try the whole figure.

A Line Can Do Anything

Move outdoors in the nice weather. There you will find a whole world of things to draw.

Always provide plenty of inexpensive paper.

Objects and Still Life

Nearly every grownup thinks of still life when he thinks of art lessons. This is an adult concept and is usually an uninspiring lesson for young people but it need not be. What most older children want to know is how to make an object look like it is on a table, not up in the air, and how to show one thing in back or in front of another. We'll concentrate on teaching that.

Getting Ready

Show the film *Discovering Perspective* the day before for demonstration (14 minutes, color—BFA, 2211 Michigan Ave., Santa Monica, CA 90904.)

One tin can

Charcoal

Large newsprint

A simple arrangement of 5 or 6 objects such as pots, dishes, fruit jars, boxes, books and cans on a table in the center of the room. Arrange the seats so each person can see it easily.

Let's Begin

"In yesterday's film on perspective how did they show one object slightly behind another? Yes, the closer one was lower on the page and overlapped the one behind it.

"We are going to make use of that idea. First let's look at this can top. It looks round when I hold it like this.

"See how it seems to change shape when I slowly tilt it up.

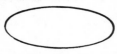 

"This is an optical illusion. The shapes you see are called ellipses. Make many ellipses with your charcoal until you can do it easily. Check to see that the edges of the ellipse are not pointed. Choose the best one and make a light horizontal guide line and a vertical one through its center.

"You will find four equal sections. When we make a jar, glass, can or similar object we will draw the entire ellipse and then darken the bottom half of both the top of the object and the bottom of the object. Connect the two vertical lines. They will be the center of your object. Now lightly draw the sides.

"Always correct your drawing so that both halves of your object are symmetrical. Draw another object behind the first one. Make a third object that is tipped over. You can turn your paper sideways to do it if that is easier for you.

"Use another piece of paper. There are five or six objects including fruit on the table. Draw the two or three that are easiest for you to see in a group. Pretend the others aren't there. Be sure to lightly sketch the ellipses and vertical lines before you make the outlines. Correct your own work. Remember how to use overlapping to show one object behind another. Draw the table lines in last. If you are drawing the fruit, figure out where to make the ellipses. With charcoal you can easily correct lines by rubbing with a tissue. Do not include any labels or printing in your drawing. Concentrate on the shapes."

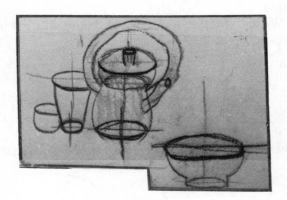

A Line Can Do Anything

How Did It Work?

"Have we corrected our own drawings?"

"Do the objects look like they are in a group with one behind another?"

"Have any of us gone one step further showing thickness of the objects?"

What Else?

Using the same criteria make collages using fabric, yarns and scrap objects for decorative wall hangings using chalk first to draw the placement of objects.

Sew an abstract design using elliptical shapes.

Use newspaper, scrap construction paper, corrugated paper or cardboard to enhance still-life drawings or designs made on cardboard or drawing paper.

Paint still-life designs with acrylics on wood as plaques.

Draw still-life pictures on newspaper with markers.

Enjoy Exaggerations

In a number of other art lessons observation and accuracy are stressed. but art, especially in this day of sophisticated camera and graphic techniques, can go a step further by the use of exaggeration. This is a natural way for children to interpret what they see, feel and hear. Once they understand what is expected, the ideas quickly emerge.

Getting Ready

Markers
Large newsprint
Newspaper desk covering

Let's Begin

"What is an exaggeration? When we make exaggerations today let's think of things that are bigger, wider, funnier or fancier than they actually look. That is really what cartoonists do instead of drawing things as they really are. Remember when we made contour drawings? We are going to make simple but clear drawings when we exaggerate.

"Take any color marker and quickly draw a chair. Now exaggerate. Pretend that some parts can be stretched or pulled wider than normal, or thinner or three times their real size. Make another chair overlapping the first but make it look funny. Make it bigger, wider, like it's overstuffed. Make it look as if you'd get lost in all the cushions on it. Put lots of designs all over it.

"Make another one. This time it should be so tall and skinny that it goes off the top of the page and off the bottom. Draw lots of stripes up and down to exaggerate the size even more. What else can you add? Try outlining it in another color. Use thick and thin lines and texture, too. Exaggerate the strange shape. See what else you can add to make this look like the most unusual chair you ever saw. Fill in some of the negative shapes to complete your design."

How Did It Work?

Does the chair design look real or exaggerated?
Are negative as well as positive forms evident?
Are there a variety of lines and textures?
Is there an all-over look or unity?

What Else?

"Cut out a piece of construction paper in an exaggerated shape like some sort of closed curve.

A Line Can Do Anything

"These can be imaginary shapes or cartoonlike drawings of people or animals. Do not use cartoons created by other people. Make up your own. Paste it on a 12″ x 18″ piece of drawing paper, but not in the center. Use markers to emphasize the shape by repeating it in larger shapes all around it until your shapes fill the page. Fill some parts in with different widths of lines."

Texture and Line

Texture in drawing is created. If the children have not had experience in making rubbings or texture collages, plan those lessons first. Have examples of textures to show them. The book *Design in Nature* is an excellent reference.

Getting Ready

Any dry medium, thick or soft pencils, charcoal or crayon can be used to create texture.
Paper—newsprint or manila drawing paper

Let's Begin

"I have a large piece of paper here and a soft pencil. Who can come and make a soft line for me? Now let's put many short, soft lines very close together. If these were something to touch what could it be?

"Fur? hair? grass?

"How could we make these lines look as if they were rough or prickly? Yes - press harder and make them farther apart!

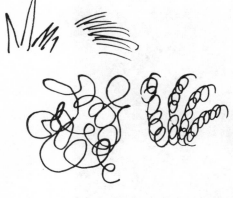

"Which line could you use for a porcupine? A bunny?

"Lots of curly lines close together are fun. Who can try this?

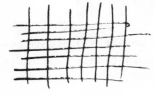

"How could we show burlap or screen?

"Let's draw several shapes that overlap on our paper. In the new shapes where you see overlapping, let's create a new texture. Try not to repeat textures —make some lines thin and close, others thick and far apart, some wiggly and some wavy."

How Did It Work?

"Are there a variety of textures? Who can see a texture in someone else's picture they'd like to try? What could we use some of these textures for in a drawing? Are we using the side as well as the point of our drawing tool?"

A Line Can Do Anything

What Else?

Bring in a large plush toy animal and put it on a shag rug. Have the children draw this.

If the weather is nice, go outdoors and look for many things to draw in one picture that show different textures. For example, brick buildings, wooden houses, grass, trees, flowers, bushes, pebbles, and anything else available.

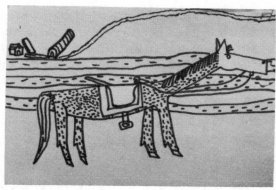

Draw imaginary creatures that have soft fur, scales or bristly whiskers.

Simple Perspective and How It Happens

When a child asks, "What's wrong with my picture? It doesn't look right," that is the time for a lesson in simple perspective. But even if a fourth grader doesn't say it out loud, he may be questioning himself. It is not necessary to talk about vanishing points to show how to make objects look as if they relate to other forms in the same picture. There are a few simple concepts that clarify perspective for adults and children alike.

Getting Ready

> Show the film *Discovering Perspective*
> Pencil
> Crayons
> 12″ x 18″ drawing paper

Let's Begin

Use the film *Discovering Perspective*, which teaches perspective in a clear, exciting way and summarizes the lesson at the end. Then write on the board or make a chart as you discuss the film with the class.

"Who can tell one way to show perspective? Overlapping is right. Yes, show one object higher and one lower. Make the closest thing with more detail and use less and less detail as each other form gets further away. Another way is to show that things in the distance appear more grey in color. Draw rows of objects so that they seem to come together at the furthest point from our eyes." This last concept is the most advanced and usually the more mature students are the ones

A Line Can Do Anything

who fully understand it. "All of these are ways to show perspective. To make things as they really are artists use several ways in the same drawing.

"Think of one object in nature or one that is manufactured that you can draw well. Use your pencil and crayons and draw it a number of times on the same paper using as many ways of showing perspective as you can."

For the youngster who can't think of anything, be encouraging. Make a suggestion for the age level or perhaps mention an object in the room that the student can draw. This is a lesson that is appropriate for all ability levels in the middle grades and higher. Each student should make a complete picture, not just a sketch.

How Did It Work?

"Which pictures have the feeling of space or distance?

"Who has used texture to show more detail and less detail?

"When illustrating the principle of overlapping, does the object in front look nearer than those higher up?

"Do things in the distance look more muted in color and form?

"Do the rows of things actually look like they are going further away or coming from the distance?"

Have any of the more advanced students made a composition or scene with the objects they have chosen?

What Else?

Have those who are able or very interested use mixed media to show perspective.

Wallpaper, fabric and cord or yarn will provide inspiration for collage work. Make rubbings to show detail or greyed areas in drawings.

Draw machinery, groups of people or gardens using the principles of perspective.

Remind the students to show perspective in all their realistic drawings now that they understand how.

4 What Makes That Mark?

"Why, drawing is done with a pencil, isn't it?" a novice might wonder. In art there is always more than one way to do anything. You can never run out of ideas, nor will the children, if you simply elaborate, try something new and innovate. Try other ways of drawing, less conventional perhaps, but very valid. String, sticks, brushes, marking pens, charcoal, crayons, chalk, and anything else you may find that can make marks are worth experimenting with. The stiff, hard points are more easily controlled, while the soft, movable drawing tools produce a freer effect.

String Drawing

What fun it is to wiggle a string soaked in black tempera and see what it can do on a large piece of paper! Thick and thin lines, bold and shy ones make all kinds of patterns. Lines created in string drawing are free and varied and cannot be done with other drawing tools.

What Makes That Mark?

Getting Ready

Desk covering
Smocks
8″ piece of string for each child
Plastic coffee can lids
Thick black tempera
Sticks
Rags
12″ x 18″ newsprint or larger
Music
Opaque projector
Drawings by Michelangelo, DaVinci, Ben Shahn, Kathe Kollwitz

Let's Begin

"Artists use line in exciting ways. Here are some of the black and white drawings by Michelangelo and Leonardo Da Vinci that look as if they might have been done yesterday. Look how lines were used. See the contrast between the white paper and the black lines. Notice how they seem to move. Can you find thick lines that slide into thinner ones? Many lines are as thin as hairs and are made so close to each other that they seem to be drawn in a big hurry. Now look at the drawings by Ben Shahn done in the 1940s and 50s. Although they are simple they, too, make use of interesting lines. Sometimes it is hard to see what was used to make them. The drawings by Kathe Kollwitz, drawn in the 1930s and 40s, were done with pencil, charcoal, crayon and brush or pen and ink.

"Today we are going to make some line drawings without worrying about the subject matter. We will use pieces of string coated with tempera paint. Then we will discover the variety of lines that can be made by moving the string freely across the paper. Move it quickly sometimes and slowly at other times. Try as many other movements with the string as you can.

"A small amount of thick, black tempera has been poured into shallow plastic lids so we can easily use a stick or our fingers to help coat the string with the black paint. Put the wet string on your paper and move it all around as the music plays. Try to use the entire paper and let your string drawing reach the edges. Overlap your lines, gather the string together and slide it around on the paper while you listen. Think of the music and invent

What Makes That Mark?

ways of making swirls, jagged lines, dots and other marks you can't make with a pencil. Turn your paper around from time to time so the painting or drawing doesn't seem too black in one place. Use another paper when one is finished. Put the first piece on the floor next to your desk to dry."

How Did It Work?

Is there a variety of lines?
Do the lines overlap?
Do they seem to move?

What Else?

Another time, use the same materials and more pictures on the opaque projector for motivation, but take the lesson one step further. See what forms or shapes seem to emerge. Emphasize them by placing lines in certain areas purposely rather than only at random. Have each picture looked at from a distance, perhaps from across the room. Hold it vertically, horizontally and upside down. Which way makes a more exciting picture?

Use different background music to inspire new string drawings.

Children in all age groups have fun gluing colored string on construction paper. Direct gluing without drawing first produces the most exciting results.

Sticks as Tools

An ideal follow-up lesson to drawing with string, where there was only a limited amount of control, is using a stick as a painting or drawing tool. By using several different sticks it is easy to get a variety of lines and textures, which artists usually achieve by skillful handling of brushes and pens (more sophisticated tools).

Getting Ready

     Several pieces of 12″ x 18″ manila paper
     Several pieces of newspaper desk covering per child (a stick might make a
          hole in thin newsprint)
     A large selection of twigs, branches, plastic mixing sticks, Popsicle sticks, etc.
     ½″ of black tempera in cans or egg cartons
     20th century drawings by
          Rico Lebrun
          A. Jorn
          Max Ernst
          Marino Marini
          Pablo Picasso (The Picador series)
          Philip Guston
          Yasuo Kunioshi
          (An excellent source is *Drawings of the Masters*, 20th Century
            Drawings, Part II, 1940 to the present, by Una E. Johnson,
            Shorewood Publishers, Inc. N.Y. 1964)
     An opaque projector

Let's Begin

    "As we looked at the drawings what did you notice about the use of lines? How did they seem to be made? Were you able to tell what the artist was thinking of even

What Makes That Mark?

though these were not realistic pictures? When we experimented with tempera and string, some of you wanted to do more than the string let you do. We will work with sticks today and you will see the difference. What kind of lines do you suppose twigs will make? What about wider sticks, Popsicle sticks, plastic mixing sticks? Some are good to use when we need wider lines. We can even use the side of a flat stick.

"Choose any one to begin with and then use another when you've found out everything the first stick can do. Hold the paper horizontally. Make large arm movements and let the stick move first slowly and then faster as it makes thick and thin lines all over the page. Turn the paper around so that all the lines don't start from one place. Work more on one section. See how the lines overlap and that area seems to be darker. When your design pleases you, stop. Take another paper. Don't wait for anyone else. This time hold your paper vertically. Try another stick or perhaps tape a thick and thin one together. This time after you have made a group of interesting lines try to get some texture. Purposely cross some of the lines so that they look like a screen. In another place make lines of different lengths and thicknesses quite close to each other. Have a friend hold your picture five or six feet away or put it on the floor next to your desk and look at it as you stand. Does it begin to remind you of something? See what ideas you can develop. Many times artists create as they work rather than sketching first."

What Makes That Mark?

How Did It Work?

Pin the line drawings on the bulletin board and let the class talk about them while viewing them at a distance of from six to ten feet. Choose three or four students to pin them up but let the artist tell which is the top.

Are the lines varied? Which pictures show use of texture, crosshatching, and new forms? Are the lines free enough to suggest new thoughts or are they still tight, unimaginative and overcontrolled?

What Else?

Use mood music, poetry or a beautifully written story for inspiration while the class is drawing.

If a painted, chalk, collage mural, or poster needs some strong outlines to liven it up, use the stick and tempera technique to add that spark.

Drawing with a Brush

Children can draw directly on paper with a brush without predrawing with a pencil if they are allowed to experiment several times with both stiff easel brushes and soft watercolor brushes. Don't worry about color at first, just use black tempera. Drawing done with a brush is fun and creative and will help you get better paintings from your class.

Getting Ready

    Shirt or smock
    Newspaper or a desk cover

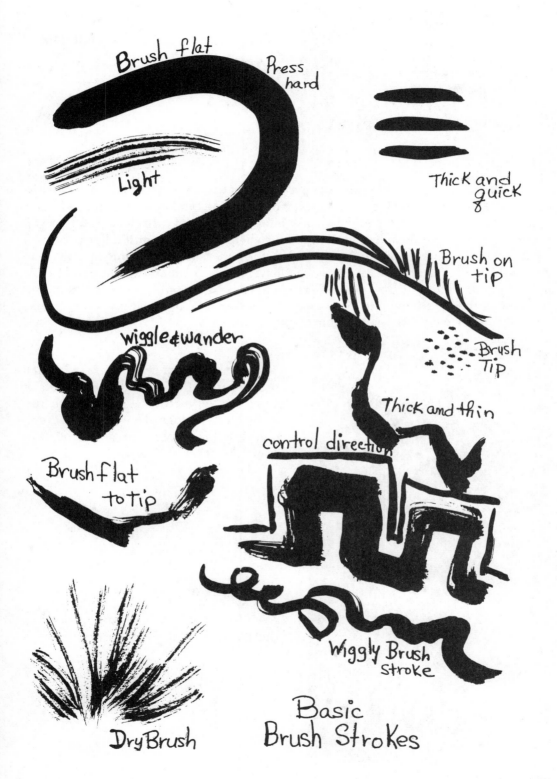

Brush flat

Press hard

Light

Thick and quick

Brush on tip

Brush Tip

wiggle & wander

Thick and thin

Brush flat to tip

control direction

Wiggly Brush stroke

Dry Brush

Basic Brush Strokes

½″ easel brushes
Black tempera
Water and rag
Several sheets of newsprint

Let's Begin

"Remember the line game we played? What were some of the lines we discovered? Today we are going to make some of those lines and new ones, too, with our stiff easel brushes. We will try some brush lines on the board with clean water (or you can use a large paper on an easel). Our brushes help us make beautiful lines. We will use big arm movements and sweep around on the paper. Who will come up and make a very thick line for us? We need to push hard on the brush and spread the bristles out to get a thick line. Now I want someone to come here and make a very thin line by keeping the brush up on its tip. Good! When we use a lot of paint we get a thick, dark line. How could we make a thin, light, soft line?

"Now start on your own paper and paint a picture using thick and thin lines, lots of paint, or very little. Remember to use many kinds of lines like we did in a drawing. Fill the paper and go all over in many directions."

How Did It Work?

Are the paintings bold and varied? Is there a great variety of line?

What Makes That Mark?

What Else?

The next lesson should be with soft bristle brushes and white paint. Compare the results the children have gotten with stiff easel brushes and soft hair brushes.

Another time use color and both kinds of brushes.

Keep plenty of paper handy and allow the children to each paint several pictures.

Tape a sheet of butcher paper on the wall and have some paints on a small, newspaper-covered table nearby. Allow children to paint on it when they have free time. Establish rules: Work here only if work is done and only two or three artists at a time, space permitting.

Magic with Markers

What's the magic? The children love to draw with markers; the colors are beautiful, and it is easy to get thick and thin lines.

Permanent markers have nice colors but the room must be well-ventilated when an entire class works with them. Watercolor markers do not have an odor, but they dry out quickly.

Felt-tipped markers are versatile because of the variety of lines that can be made by using the different surfaces of the felt tip.

Getting Ready

A covering for desk (*most important* because most markers are permanent)
12″ x 18″ or larger white drawing paper

Let's Begin

"You know how to draw so well by now that today we shall have a special treat. We are going to draw with markers on large paper.

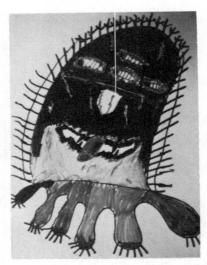

"We will make a creature no one has ever seen before. That means we won't make Frankenstein's monster, the Wolf Man or a dinosaur you've seen before. Your creature may have many different animal parts, or be half man, half animal, or it may have eighteen legs or three heads, one eye or five eyes, but it will be your creation and not like anyone else's. Can it have fangs? Yes, anything you wish. We will make our creatures so large they fill the entire page. Don't forget to try textures, too."

How Did It Work?

The children will enjoy this evaluation because the results are always great! Is each creature unique? Imaginative? Colorful? Textured? Big? etc.

What Else?

Try marker drawings over:

Acrylic paints (see chapter 5)
Tissue collage (see chapter 5)

What Makes That Mark?

Watercolor washes (see chapter 5)
Accent and texture tempera paintings

Divide a 6″ x 9″ piece of manila paper into areas with straight or curved lines using a black marker.

Color areas, then add texture with lighter or darker colored markers.

Charcoal Rather Than Pencil*

"That's great. It gives me the feeling of being scooped up into the air. When I look at it, these lines grab hold of me and pull me with it."

The medium is charcoal. The group is asked to break the sticks into two or three sections, each about two inches long. We are going to use charcoal in a free, flowing way to encourage fifth and sixth grade students to use the entire arm rather than the tight finger movements they have become so used to. Many of the children at this age try too hard to be exact in drawing and are actually afraid of making "mistakes." There are no mistakes in art.

Getting Ready

    Charcoal
    12″ x 18″ manila paper
    Music or poetry reading as background
    (Optional) inexpensive hair spray as fixative—use outdoors or in a well-ventilated area

*From "Flow with Charcoal," Barbara Tuch, *Arts and Activities*, December 1972, p. 25. Used by permission of the publisher.

What Makes That Mark?

Let's Begin

This is an exciting lesson, especially when the students have just come to school braving a blizzard or a wind or sleet storm. It can be saved for a blustery day or even a particularly dull one. When bad weather sets the mood, just a few words re-create the tone. Music or poetry helps out in other instances.

"How did you feel crossing the street in all that wind? Take your charcoal, hold it sideways, and pretend it is the movement of the wind. Sweep it across the page. Make it go all around. Again, now again. Let it go off the page. Now bring it back in. Small, light scraps are flying around. Make them. Something is smashed against a wall. BANG!!! Now the wind has died down and things have settled peacefully. Take your second piece of paper and place it on top of the first.

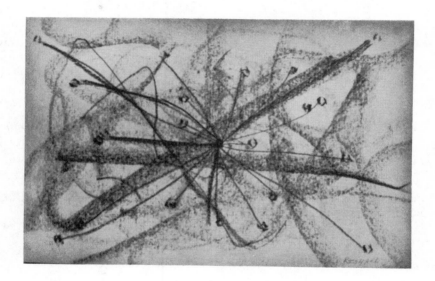

"Everything is calm now. Nothing seems to be happening. In fact, it is too quiet . . . . eerie. The air is waiting, still, as if something is about to happen. Show that. Take a soft piece of charcoal. See the textures that makes? Add something strange."

Instruct the group to take the third piece of paper. Don't hesitate at this point.

"Sounds are coming closer and closer. Show that. Swing your charcoal around; use the edge for emphasis. Make one part of your picture clear. Try turning the paper around. Focus your attention on the most important area. Add details. What shapes are starting to emerge? Emphasize them. Overlap lines and shapes. Add texture. There you are!"

How Did It Work?

End the lesson with enough time left for class discussion. Lay the drawings on the floor, and let the group discuss what it sees.

What Else?

Go one step further in a second charcoal lesson. Use free arm motion and then turn the pictures around and let imaginations wander. Accent emerging shapes or forms. Darken others.

What Makes That Mark?

Crayon Resist—A New Way

An ecology-minded teacher can find a use for everything. Save the carbon sheet from dittos and thermofax for a lesson combining line drawing and crayon resist. The wax crayon repels the ditto ink when the drawing is dipped in water, hence the term "resist."

Getting Ready

> White or manila drawing paper
> A sharp pencil or ballpoint pen
> Crayons
> Carbonlike sheets from ditto masters
> Newspaper to dry drawings on
> Sink or flat pans of water

Let's Begin

"Today we are going to create some 'magic drawings.' Do you know what this purple paper is used for? We will place the carbonlike side of the purple paper under our white drawing paper. With your pen or pencil make a line drawing on paper of a

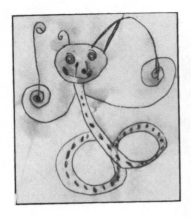
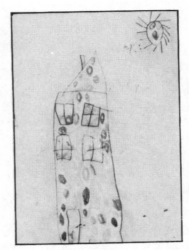

bird, animal or insect no one has ever seen before. Remember to use all the kinds of lines we've been learning about so that your creation is furry, spiny, scaly, or to make the world it lives in fantastic. When your drawing is completed, put the carbonlike paper back on the pile on my desk. Turn your drawing over and crayon the areas you want to color. Press very hard. When you have your crayoned areas finished, go to the sink and run cold water over your drawing letting the colored ink run as much as you like. Put your picture on the newspapers to dry."

How Did It Work?

This lesson interests the children and they enjoy doing several drawings. Discuss the dreamy, other-worldlike effect the ink creates when it is washed. Which drawings have the most interesting lines, and which drawings are most imaginative?

What Else?

Try drawing pictures of outer space—imaginary spaceships, people, plants and worlds. Draw scenes of underwater life in conjunction with an oceanography unit.

Another new way for resist—Draw with the stubs of old wax candles in white or a light color. The drawing is invisible until the watercolor or ink is washed over the surface.

What Makes That Mark?

Chalk

Chalk lines have a special sparkly quality that you and the children will enjoy. Learning to work with chalk and keeping it smudge-free requires some experimenting. This lesson can help.

Getting Ready

> White or manila paper
> Colored chalks, prebroken into small pieces
> Covering for desk

Let's Begin

"We will take a piece of chalk between our thumb and fingers so we can rub its flat side on our paper. Put the chalk down and look at the line. What do you like about it? How is it different from a painted or marker-drawn line?

"Chalk work is soft and fuzzy. The paper you are working on should sparkle through the chalk color. Try other colors and lines, overlapping and using as much space on your paper as you can. What happens when colors meet?

"How can we get darker thin lines? Use your chalk like a pencil to draw more details."

How Did It Work?

"Who had the most interesting use of line? Does anyone see a possibility for another drawing? Why do you or don't you like chalk as a drawing tool?"

What Else?

Wet a paper towel (the heavy brown school type). Draw on it with chalk. When it is dry mount it on construction paper and coat it with polymer.* This makes a permanent drawing and the polymer deepens the chalk colors. Try using chalk on a Styrofoam tray that has just been brushed with polymer.

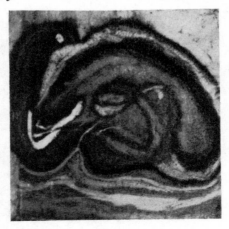

---

*When applying polymer, daub each color area separately with a stiff easel brush. Do not stroke back and forth from one color to another because the colors will smear.

5 Every Child Loves a Rainbow

Capture the rainbow colors coming through a prism in your sunlit classroom and you will capture your class's attention. Children love to find their favorite colors in the rainbow and they enjoy reproducing rainbow colors on paper with watercolor paints. Another favorite color activity is to look at each other's brightly colored clothing and then take turns walking into a darkened closet and see the color almost disappear and then reappear as the child walks out into the light. Experiments in light and color can be this easy and this much fun.

Children think of color, moods and feelings together. Talk to your class about their ideas of color. "What is your favorite color? Why?" Most children love oranges and yellows and will associate these colors with the sun, warmth, or sometimes happiness. A child's response to red may be surprising. While some may think of it as gay or exciting, others may feel that red is anger, blood, pain or fire. Black, purple and blues are usually related to night, darkness, sadness or quiet. Encourage the children to use colors in paintings and drawings to express feelings of their own.

"Look, I made avocado!" When a tiny, five-year-old Michelangelo, in his oversize painting shirt, spouts this poetic thought as he dabbles in his first kindergarten watercolor experience, you must realize that he has a sophisticated color background. Color comes so naturally to children that it is best to approach teaching color to youngsters by tossing out most traditional methods.

Park the color wheels in the closet! Words such as value, hue and shade are not necessary now!

If learning is free and experimental, children will discover that colors can be changed. Sometimes red, for example, becomes light (pink), or almost orange. Telling another how their various colors are made is a triumph for the color creator.

Temperas, acrylics or watercolor paints can be used successfully with any age group if adult methods and techniques are not imposed upon the children.

If a child uses color freely, easily and with conviction, if he likes to experiment and create new ways to use color, then his learning process has been successful. He has found a new tool to use in the future, and this is what every learning experience should do.

Let's look at ways to explore the wonderful world of color!

WET MEDIA IN COLOR

Water

"It's too early in the year to paint. The children don't even know their colors." These are some of the best reasons for the preschool or kindergarten teacher to start her class painting with water. The price is right and warm weather is perfect for a first painting experience.

Getting Ready

> A bucket of water
> Water containers for each child—an orange juice can is fine
> Large easel-type flat brushes—#10
> A nice day

Tell the children that they are going outside, but not for recess and not to go home. Everyone is going to paint an invisible picture, a picture that will disappear. There will be brushes and everyone can dip for his own water from a bucket.

Where is the paint? There isn't any. That's the fun. Imaginations can easily blossom.

Let's Begin

Have the children carry out all the empty cans and brushes in a bag or basket. There should be one for each. You carry the bucket half filled with water. Find out if there is an outdoor faucet or hose that could be used for refills. Explain how each one will paint the sidewalk with water. The sidewalk will look black for a few minutes wherever the water goes. Then the pictures will disappear. Have everyone make dots and splashes, lines and wiggles. Each boy or girl works in his own special space. Everyone takes a can and dips it into the bucket, getting his or her own water. One child distributes the brushes. A space is given to each little person and the painting begins. If water spills, no reprimand is necessary. To end the lesson simply collect the brushes and spill the remaining water on the grass.

Every Child Loves a Rainbow

What Else?

Next time the class can paint inside using one or two colors on 18″ x 24″ newsprint.

Finger Paints

Many of us avoid finger painting because it is "messy," "too much trouble" or because of lack of experience with it. Since it is an exciting way to paint and great fun, here are some suggestions to help you enjoy a finger painting session with your class.

Getting Ready

Stack all the chairs at the side of the room—you'd be surprised how necessary
   this is!
Finger paint and finger paint paper
Large, flat pans half-filled with water (plastic tote trays are fine)
Small plastic bowls half filled with water
Large newspaper sheets carefully spread on the floor for paintings to dry on
Wastepaper basket
Smocks—the sleeves should be rolled up or cut off above the elbow
Rags (preferably) or sponges
Plastic spoons
Soap
Music
Mothers or older children help set up and clean up

Have the children sit on the floor and do the hand motions suggested below.

Wet the desks or table tops with water from small bowls with sponges. Pass
each sheet of finger paint paper through the water in the flat pan. Don't soak, but wet
thoroughly.

Smooth a sheet of wet paper at each place
using a sponge or rag and put about one
tablespoon of finger paint on each one.
Keep a separate spoon for each color.

One helper will remove each finished
finger painting and put it on the newspaper to dry while another wets and puts
fresh paper down.

Let's Begin

"Do you remember when we went outside and painted without any paint?
Today we are going to paint without any brushes. Our fingers and hands will be our
brushes.

"How many boys and girls can move their hands like this in the air? Let's
make believe we are pushing the paint all over the paper so none of the white shows
anymore. Now see if you can move both hands in big circles. Can your circles go the
other way? Pretend it is raining. Show how the rain falls and splatters on the ground.

"Where is the side of your hand? Wiggle it back and forth like a snake. Make a
fist by closing all your fingers. Move your hands up and back, toward you and away
from you. What else can we do with our hands? Show us.

Every Child Loves a Rainbow

"At each table another color of finger paint has been used. What color is on this table? What color is here? . . . .

"Here are the people who will work at the red table. These boys and girls will paint at the blue table. . . . .

"Now we'll begin. Spread the paint all over your paper. Use both hands. Let's make some big circles first. Try some little ones. How about zigzags like lightning? Now raindrops. Oh, see them coming down faster and faster. But look, the rain is stopping. The worms are coming out. Move your hands like they move. Let's go fishing. See how rough the water is today. Make the waves with the side of your hand. Now let's erase our pictures. Use your whole hand. Now use all your fingers together. Can you spread your fingers apart and make lots of lines at the same time? See what else you can make. Try to make lots of funny marks. Make your own painting."

Music could be played to inspire rhythm and movement in the pictures.

Have the helpers lift each finished painting by the corners, placing them on the newspapers to dry. Have the next paper ready. The children who are finished can work at the adjoining table with a new color. Hands should *not* be washed until the second painting is finished.

Leave plenty of time for cleanup. One helper wipes each child's hands with a rag and another stands at the sink helping wash the hands.

The children who are washed may quietly read a book or sit and listen to the music while the others are finishing.

Children of all ages enjoy finger painting so don't limit this experience to kindergarten or first grade.

How Did It Work?

Did the boys and girls use a variety of hand and finger motions? Were they able to see imaginary forms and develop them further? Were they willing to "erase" the designs or pictures and make more? Was this an enjoyable experience?

What Else?

For a second finger painting lesson, finger paint directly on a Formica surface and lay the finger paint paper on top to lift a print of the painting. This produces an entirely different look and texture and eliminates the need to prepare the paper on the tables. Murals can be made in this way, too.

Using the paintings: The interesting movements and textures in finger painting make an attractive background for bulletin boards.

    Book binding: Paste finger paintings to cardboard with Metylan for attractive covers for the children's original stories.

    Multimedia: Use the finger paintings as background and apply cut paper shapes or figures. Mount poetry or short stories on the finger painting.

Watercolor Paints

    "It's fuzzy!" "It's like an explosion!" "This paint wiggles!" "Look at my beautiful new color!"

Every Child Loves a Rainbow

Children react in these ways to watercolor because it is wonderful, wet and experimental. Watercolor sets for young children usually come in small boxes with a versatile little brush. A set that only has the three primary colors (red, yellow and blue) and black will give you more paint and more freedom to mix beautiful colors. The paints must be wet to be used. The first lessons will be guided to give the children some ways to use the paint and brush. From then on, there is no end to the surprises and beauty the children can find with watercolors.

Getting Ready

> A shirt or smock for each child
> Paper towels or painting rags
> Water in cans for each child
> A cover for the desk
> Three or four sheets of white or manila drawing paper for each child
> Watercolor paints and brush in boxes
> (*Optional, but great!*) two plastic buckets on newspaper in middle of work
>   area—one empty for dirty water and one filled with clean water for
>   filling cans.

Let's Begin

"We are going to work with paints called watercolors. Water is very important as you work today. Do you like water? What is nice about it? (Hoped-for responses: It is fun to play in, wet, shiny, clear, etc.) We can see through water and these colors will be like this on your paper.

"Let's all take our brushes and dip them in our clean water. Drop or squeeze the clear water on the red, yellow and blue colors. Do not touch the brush on the colors yet.

"Let's thoroughly wet some parts of our paper and leave some parts dry. Now choose one of the colors you wet and sweep the brush across the paper.

"What happened? Some parts (the wet ones) are fuzzy. Some parts (the dry ones) have lines that have clear, sharp edges and show the paper sparkling through. The wet areas are called washes and the dry areas are called dry brush.

"Now take another color and sweep it across the paper and let it meet the first color in some places. What happened? Where colors meet, a new color is mixed.

"Go on and finish your painting and discover all the things you can do with paints.

"There is no white paint in watercolors, so you must leave the paper untouched to get white areas."

Walk about and help the children to work quickly and freely. Help them to avoid "scrubbing" the paper by painting over and over in one area. If they see bubbles and bits of paper flecking the paint, they are overbrushing.

How Did It Work?

Encourage the children to exhibit their pictures and comment on good watercolor techniques such as use of washes, line, and beautiful new colors.

What Else?

Allow the children to have many opportunities to paint with watercolors.

Topics for paintings—Landscapes with color washes for background, marker-drawn buildings, trees, hills over the background. Action drawings of people. Water scenes with boats, fish, or underwater painting are naturals with water paints. Try clowns or pictures of a rainy day.

Incidentally, watercolor paints are fine to use for crayon resist because they are transparent.

Every Child Loves a Rainbow

Powder Paints

Some schools have both powder paints and tempera in jars. Powder paint can be mixed with water using a long stick until it is the consistency of heavy cream. Store it in jars and use it as regular tempera. But, how about doing something different?

Getting Ready

Desk covering, smocks, water containers, rags or sponges
12″ x 18″ drawing paper used on a flat desk or table
½″ stiff bristle easel brushes
Metylan art paste—premix
Cans of powder paint
Popsicle sticks
Egg cartons to hold paint and paste
Arrange tables so children can work in small groups and share equipment

Let's Begin

"Have you ever heard the wind howling and scattering things all about? Your brush will be the wind and the paint will represent all the trees, boxes, paper and people that are being tossed all over by the ferocious blowing. Think of how it feels to be pushed by the wind. Show how it shoves everything in its path. Take your brush, dip it into the Metylan paste and swoop it across the page. Now dip the brush into the powder paint. Get lots on your brush and swish it across on top of the paste. Paint quickly. Choose another color and try again.

"When that picture is finished, we'll try a different idea. Use a Popsicle stick to sprinkle a bit of powder paint onto your paper. Let a few drops of water fall on the paint.

"Spread it with your brush. What does it look like? Can you get different textures? Does the Metylan help you get a smooth surface? Use the dry sponge or rag now. Dip it into some of the powder paint. Now dot it on your paper. Add some water with your brush. Try some more experiments."

How Did It Work?

"Are the paintings dry? Does the paste make the paint dry faster or more slowly? How can we use that idea?"

What Else?

Why not combine powder tempera with water and Metylan in an egg carton and use it to paint 3-D art work?

Still another time use the powder paint on top of a collage or as a background for one. Or create an interesting pastel background, adding tempera for accents. Use a marker to print an original haiku poem or other verse upon it.

If you have no finger paint, try making some with Metylan and the powder paint mixed to the consistency of gelatin. Use it on shiny paper.

Did you know you can create an interesting feeling of depth or texture by adding sand or tiny paper circles from the hole puncher, or sawdust, coffee grounds or pencil shavings to the paste-paint mixture?

Tempera Paints

Tempera, often called poster paint, is an opaque, water-based paint. It is sometimes packed in dry, powder form in shaker-type cans or ready-mixed in jars, preferably in plastic squeeze bottles. The consistency is quite thick and should be applied with ½-inch or wider long-handled brushes. It can be thinned with water, if necessary.

The colors flow easily and dry without a gloss. Colors can be applied on top of one another. Sometimes mixed tempera colors are not as true as those found in mixed watercolors. A green made from blue and yellow tempera may be a gray-green, rather than the clear, crisp green produced from the same watercolors, so choose the right paint for the job!

Getting Ready

Each child will need:
A place to work—an easel, a desk or the floor, well covered with oilcloth or
    newspapers
A can for water
Jars for paint at easel; plastic egg cartons at desks

Every Child Loves a Rainbow

A smock or painting shirt
A paper towel or cloth
A place to dry paintings
Several pieces of paper such as newsprint or manila—12″ x 18″ or 18″ x 24″.

Let's Begin

"Today we will use tempera paint. Have you ever painted with tempera? Did you enjoy it? Why? Watch me dip the brush into the paint. Does it drip? No! This is because it is very thick. There are many nice, new shapes and colors we can create with tempera. Try new things as you work. Who can tell us how to get a thick line with the brush? How could we paint a soft, fuzzy texture? Our first paintings can be just colors, lines, shapes and textures."

How Did It Work?

If the children do more than one picture, have each select his favorite and put the gallery of paintings up where everyone can see. Encourage self-evaluation or group discussions that are positive and helpful to everyone. Do the children work freely? Are they using clear, bright colors and a variety of brush strokes and shapes?

What Else?

Tempera paint can be mixed with polymer for more permanency. An addition of dishwashing detergent improves adherence to other media such as glass or plastic containers.

Large murals are exciting and can be permanent displays for school corridors and stairways when mounted or painted on cardboard. Quite often murals can be an important part of social studies or science work. This is a fine way for an upper elementary group to leave a memento to their school.

Try tempera on:

Burlap, old sheets, fabrics
Paper bags
Three-dimensional projects
Marblex clay
Crayon resist
Scraffito

Acrylic Paints

There is a new paint that is fun and easy to use for those very special painting projects. Acrylics are synthetic paints that are smooth and spread easily over many kinds of surfaces. They come in a wide range of beautiful colors and are water-soluble. Acrylics mix with other water-soluble media, such as powdered tempera, and can be thinned with water if necessary. Acrylics are permanent and *waterproof* when dry. What does this mean?

Wash the brushes immediately!
Wipe up spills and spots immediately!
Cover working surfaces!
Wear smocks

Why should you use acrylics?

They dry quickly!
They do not chip off easily!
They are a permanent surface
  for many projects

Every Child Loves a Rainbow

Getting Ready

> A shirt or smock
> A place to work
> Brushes and paints in suitable disposable containers
> Something to paint
> A can of water
> Towels or rags

Let's Begin

Acrylics are used just like tempera paints. Since they are expensive, use acrylics for special work on posters, paintings, murals, scenery, rock painting, Styrofoam painting or on wood, metal, glass and plastic. Other times use temperas. Acrylics will easily cover three-dimensional projects with less chipping and sliding.

"How can we give our projects a special finish? We will use a new, wonderful kind of paint called acrylics. They are used like temperas.

"The colors can be blended, lightened and darkened in the same way we use color with tempera paint."

NOTE: If you use Acrylic Modular Colors, this does not apply. Use these as directions indicate.

"Acrylic paint is special in another way—water does not hurt it when it is dry. We must clean our brushes and spills the minute we are through painting.

"If you want to put a light color on a dark color or paint over in any way, add patterns or textures, wait until the first color has dried, then add any color you wish."

How Did It Work?

Children will like the smooth feel of the paint as it goes on the surface and when it is dry. Encourage evaluation and decide if more work should be done on dried paint surfaces.

What Else?

Use acrylics in combination with collage.
Paint puppets
Acrylics can be used as a background. Paint, cut and paste, or use markers on top of the acrylic painting.
Rock painting.
Paint wall murals in the library, classroom and hall areas (with permission).

Markers

"Can we use markers?" is often heard when there is a choice of art media. Most children love them. They slip and slide on paper and come in beautiful colors. Markers are simple to use, easy to store and fun to work with. Some are the watercolor type, which comes off hands and clothing with soap and others are permanent. Both have their uses.

Felt-tip markers come in round, flat and angled shapes and in a variety of widths. The inch-wide refillables are a new-found tool for chart making and bulletin board titles. With a few minutes of practice, your wide lettering can be a pleasure to look at and read, even from the back of the room. Try it.

The thin, reed-type markers are handy for underlining and quick sketching. Angled markers can make lines of varied widths.

Getting Ready

Thick newspaper desk covering
Finger paint paper—variety of sizes
Permanent markers—several for each child
One large coffee can for storage of markers
Adequate ventilation—open windows
Shirts or smocks

Every Child Loves a Rainbow

Let's Begin

"How many of you have never used markers? Did you notice when the cap comes off there is a special place to put it, right on the end of the pen? There is a colored liquid inside that you can use to make great designs and pictures but it dries up very quickly. Each time you put the pen down, please cover it.

"See if you can swoop your pen around on your paper without lifting it. Can you make wide lines going into thin ones and then slide again still keeping your pen down? Remember when we did the same thing with a paintbrush? See how the line seems to move.

"What else can you make your line do?

"Choose three colors and make a picture or design covering most of your paper. Use thick and thin lines."

How Did It Work?

"Look at the shiny effect. The colors seem to glow on the finger paint paper because of its special surface. Do you like the glossy effect? Another time we'll use the watercolor markers on newsprint paper. You'll see the difference. How do you think we can use these designs?

"Did you remember to cover your markers and put them back into the coffee can with the top up so we can see the color and make sure none have lost their cover? I like the way you used the markers to change the color of the paper.

"Look at the use of negative and positive shapes. See how the design fills the space all the way to the edges.

"It's lucky we had the newspaper underneath. These markers bled right through the paper in some places."

What Else?

Coordinate art and social studies—use Indian, Mexican, Aztec or other cultural studies.

Example: "Today we'll use cotton or linen fabric. We can make curtains for our room. You can see the section I have marked off for each of you with a pencil.

We'll use the permanent markers today so the fabric will be washable. Try not to get the ink on your clothing or hands. It doesn't come off. Commercial laundries use these markers so they can identify things without worrying if the mark will disappear.

"In our study of the Aztec culture, we looked at their designs and symbols. Let's try to use the same type of markings on our fabric. Choose the colors that go with your design. Cover the entire rectangle with your markers letting the shapes go right up to the edge. Make them large and clear."

More uses for markers:

Calligraphy	Markers on papier-mâché
Designs on rocks	Charts
Styrofoam decoration	Outlining
Maps	Identification tags

OTHER MEDIA IN COLOR

Construction Paper

Your school may have a very limited art budget but one of the art materials considered essential and therefore always purchased is colored construction paper.

Every Child Loves a Rainbow

Everyone likes the bright colors but don't forget the muted ones. Contrast in art is essential for effective results.

Getting Ready

>Desk covering
>Glue or Metylan paste
>12″ x 18″ muted colors of construction paper
>Old scrap box full of odds and ends of construction paper
>Left-over ends of yarn
>Blackboard chalk
>Good scissors

"That scrap box has been getting pretty full. You really have been saving some of the most interesting shapes. You may find just the right one for the design we will be making today but if you don't, just change it. You can cut it or tear it, crumple it or bend it. Be sure to have some very large shapes along with the smaller ones. Sometimes we seem to forget that a huge shape, perhaps in the background, can help your eyes hold the entire design together."

Let's Begin

"Choose a color scheme using paper from the scrap box and get one 12″ x 18″ piece from the table. Pick one color as the most important or main one. You will use larger pieces of the main color so that it will be more important than the others. Find three or four others that seem to look interesting together. If you need other shapes for your design, plan to change the scraps by cutting or tearing.

"Draw a very large outline with chalk on your 12″ x 18″ paper. Make it a simple shape without too many wiggles and keep it as big as possible. You can easily rub the chalk off if you need to change the outline. Check with me before you cut it out. Arrange the small scrap shapes on top of the largest one without gluing them. See how many different arrangements you can make. Remember to overlap some of the pieces, have others just touching, and some all alone. Turn the design around, turn it again. Which way is the most interesting? When you have the best design, glue it down.

"Perhaps you may want to try some yarn to connect some of the shapes. If it doesn't make it look better, take it off!"

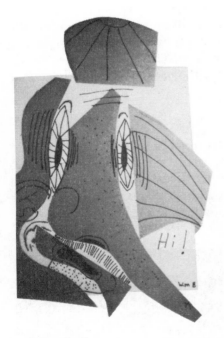

How Did It Work?

Has the class learned to choose a color scheme?

Is there a main color in each design?

Are the shapes varied in size? Interesting? Do some overlap or relate to others?

Does the design seem to hold together?

Who has used the construction paper innovatively?

Have the children really experimented with the shapes before gluing them down?

Are the students beginning to learn self-evaluation?

What Else?

3-D designs using strips in varied widths
Markers on construction paper
Masks
Crayon resist
Murals (see chapter 6)
Weaving (see chapter 7)
Ripped newspaper on construction paper
Mosaics

Every Child Loves a Rainbow

Tissue Paper

Color wheels, color theories and "how to mix what" by memory rhymes are all unnecessary if a few experimental art lessons are given to children.

Getting Ready

> Desk covering
> Orange juice cans
> Mixture of half white glue and half water in a pitcher
> Large watercolor brushes and soap to wash them
> Assorted colors of tissue paper precut on a paper cutter in various sizes and
>> shapes
> Large, flat box
> 12″ x 18″ construction paper, one for each student
> Plastic food wrap cut into lengths slightly larger than the paper

Children of all ages and their teachers, too, are successful in experimenting with color using pieces of colored tissue paper that have been previously cut into various geometric sizes and shapes and placed into a box for easier handling.

Let's Begin

"We'll each choose a color scheme. Remember to make one color the main color by choosing more of it.

"Put the plastic wrap on the desk with the construction paper on top. Fold the edges over the ends and press them down with your fingers. Turn the paper over so that the plastic wrap is on top.

"You will need about an inch of the glue and water mixture in your orange juice can. Did you know that when the glue dries on the plastic it will be practically invisible? Brush some glue on first and then take one of the larger pieces of tissue and put it on the sticky surface. Smooth it out with the wet brush. Sometimes the color of the tissue will smear. You can easily wipe your brush off on the newspaper so the glue in the can stays white. See if you can let your brush do most of the work moving the tissue to the place where you want it. Try to keep your fingers dry today. It will be easier to work that way.

"Choose another colored shape and place it slightly overlapping the first piece using your gluey brush. It doesn't matter if you put the glue on top or underneath. See what happens as you add more colors to cover the plastic wrap.

"Remove the construction paper and hold the tissue-covered plastic to the window. You will see a sea of colors."

How Did It Work?

"Wow! Do you see what happened? Look at the color I've made." "How did you get that green?" "Did you see the texture I've got?" "It looks like stained glass. If we all hang them together, it really will be beautiful."

And they will!

Cut off the excess plastic or cut the rectangle into a more unusual shape. Use Metylan glue to attach the designed pieces to the window. Every day will look bright and sunny through your "stained glass" partition.

Every Child Loves a Rainbow

What Else?

Make underwater scenes or rock crystal type formations or views of a far-away world. Let your imagination soar.

Add marker drawings on top.

Torn tissue paper collage.

Chalks and Craypas

Chalks and craypas are soft drawing and rubbing tools. Chalk can smear easily, but with more than one experience learning to use it the drawings will have a special look and the colors will be beautiful. Craypas are oil-based chalks that come in exciting colors. Children like so many to choose from.

Chalks and craypas can be used like crayons for creating large, bold color areas by holding the piece on its side and rubbing across the paper. The colors can be overlapped to create new shades and tones. They can be held like a pencil to add line details or to draw over color areas. The paper will sparkle through the colors if they are not rubbed with fingers or smeared with arms.

Getting Ready

Sets of chalk or Craypas—pieces should be unwrapped

Compartmented boxes—one section for each color—the boxes can be stored, stacked and then placed at tables for quick use

Smocks

Manila paper or white paper (several sheets)

A newspaper cover for working surface

Music—background motivation with strong rhythms such as the *Nutcracker Suite, Danse Macabre,* or the *Peer Gynt Suite.*

Let's Begin

"You have a special box on your table today. What is inside? Beautiful colored chalk pieces. Let's pick up any color. How can we hold it so that we can use the side of the chalk? We will not use the chalk like a pencil yet. Rub a shape on your paper. Do you still see the paper you covered sparkling through the chalk here and there? If we do not smear the chalk, we will always see the paper a little. Now try another color shape. Let it overlap the first one somewhere. Cover the paper with shapes and add lines that zigzag, wiggle, waver or turn sharp corners. Let the music help your arms draw the movement you hear in the music.

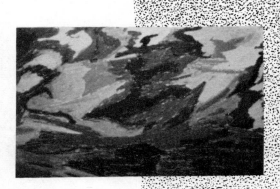

"When the paper is covered, try using dark colors on light ones, and draw on top the shapes if you wish. If you want to use thin lines, you can hold the chalk like a pencil."

How Did It Work?

Are the colors clear and bright? Are there interesting shapes and inventive use of detail? Are the children using a variety of lines to create movement? Have an evaluation and see if the children like their work or see ways to improve it.

Every Child Loves a Rainbow

What Else?

Chalk on dark construction paper—this enhances the brilliance of the chalk colors.

Chalk drawing on wet burlap or fabric.

Craypas—Since these are oil-based chalks, they can be used as a resist for paints and ink. They are not water-soluble so pieces dropped on the floor must be cleaned up quickly.

Craypas scraffito (scratch-out technique)—Colors can be overlaid and the top color can be scraped through to reveal the color underneath.

Crayons

Beautiful crayon work can rival any art media so the common crayon is one of your most versatile art tools.

Let's rediscover crayons!
Use our own imagination with crayons!
Forget coloring books, dittos, and staying within lines!

Encourage the boys and girls to use all the crayons from last year, unwrapping and breaking them in half if they are whole, because this is how crayons come into their own as an art medium. Save boxes of discarded crayons to use and get some partitioned boxes. Colors can be separated and put into the boxes to end long searches for one particular color.

A crayon is not a pencil and should not be held like one unless you need a strong line from the tip. Hold the crayon on its side to push and rub, building up layers of color; press hard for brilliance, rub lightly for fragile, subtle colors. Loosen up! Think of hundreds of ways you and the children can use crayons.

Getting Ready

> A generous supply of unwrapped, broken crayons
> An assortment of paper—newsprint
> > > manila paper
> > > white drawing paper
> > > colored construction paper

Let's Begin

"We are going to try some new ways to use our crayons today. How do crayon colors look best? How can you make the colors thick and bright? Can we use crayons to create very light colors? Try rubbing several crayons over the paper at one time. Can you mix crayon colors together?

"Let's hold the crayons flat against the paper to cover a big area quickly. Try rubbing thick lines. We will only use the crayon as a pencil when we need thin lines. It is a surprise to take your scissors and scratch lines into some crayons. What happens when you do this?

"Try crayons on several kinds of paper. See how crayons sparkle on dark and light construction paper."

How Did It Work?

Do you see signs that the children are loosening up and trying new techniques? Talk it over with the children as their work is displayed. Who found new ways to use crayons? Who has the nicest colors? Why? Do the children like the results? Do they see new ideas they'd like to try?

Every Child Loves a Rainbow

What Else?

Rubbings—The flat side of a crayon is rubbed over paper placed over real or found textures.

Scraffito—Build up thick, dark layers of crayon color on cardboard. The scratch technique, or scraffito, is done on this surface. Cover with black India ink, if available, or with thick, black crayon. Scratch into surface with round objects, scissors or compass points to reveal color underneath.

Resists—Light or dark tempera colors or watercolors over crayon. The wax in the crayons resists the wet media. Pretest the tempera over the crayons that you will use. Not all brands of tempera or crayons produce a resist effect. If the crayons do not resist the tempera, use a cheaper, waxier crayon. If the tempera cracks, thin it with water first.

Crayon first, then paint over all with tempera. Quickly wash the painting under the water faucet to remove some of the paint. Watercolor paint brushed over crayon work produces yet another effect and does not need to be washed.

Textures—Create crosshatching lines, scribbling, short strokes, long wavy lines, and curly lines by experimenting with various crayon surfaces.
Shaved crayons—Use on wet acrylic or tempera areas or on white glue.
Crayon—Use on wood.
Crayon and marker—For drawings and designs.
Crayon—On finger paint, or try finger paint over a crayon picture.

Crayon—On dry tempera paintings.

On construction paper—Try reds on grey or blues on yellow and other color combinations.

On fabric—muslin (crayon colors can be melted with a warm iron. Put fabric between sheets of newspaper before using iron.)

On burlap.

Silkscreen—Use crayon as the resist areas.

Chunk-o-crayon—Blocks of commercially prepared multicolored crayon chips can be used for unusual effects.

6 Planning Painless Painting: It Can Be So Easy

Paint sometimes stays on the shelf year after year. There is no reason to avoid using this medium. Every classroom from kindergarten to the upper grades should have easels or tables always available for painting and in use. The whole class does not have to paint at the same time. Children develop their own painting techniques through the years if they are encouraged to use the brushes and paint often. After a few introductory lessons trying various sizes and types of brushes, mixing colors and learning how each kind of paint can be used, let the children paint by themselves and clean up when they have free time. You will see that some children use bold brush strokes and strong colors. Others have a good sense of design and use line effectively. There will be children who create delicate work with great detail. These children are learning to paint.

Easel Painting

You should insist on having several double-faced easels in your room. Place them in a corner near the sink. Buy several yards of heavy plastic material to cover the floor. This can be taped so that it stays where you want it. Have painting shirts available on hooks near the sink or on the side of the easel. Keep plenty of rags for wiping brushes and spills, as well as soap, paper towels and large sponges near the sink. Provide coffee cans partially filled with water in the sink to soak the brushes. Have extra cans on a windowsill or table nearby to dry them. Keep the bristles up at all times to avoid breaking or bending them.

Paint can be kept in the easel tray in jars or cans with lids. When more paint is needed, teach the children to add it from large squeeze bottles of tempera. At the end of each day, the cleanup committee should fill jars, wipe the lip of each jar, and cap and close them. A small amount of "Vaseline" Petroleum Jelly keeps the lids from sticking. Wash the brushes thoroughly and dry them overnight. Now and then you could ask the room mother to wash the shirts and paint rags for you.

Prepare the easel with paper. Begin with several sheets of newspaper, then have as many large sheets of paper clipped to the easel as the clips will hold.

Have a drying rack, newspapers on the floor under tables or a clothesline and clips handy to dry the paintings. When the work is dry it can be taken home or left in a designated place to use in classroom displays. Each child should learn to carefully unclip his or her own work of art and set it out to dry.

Have a supply of markers or scrap paper and glue nearby if the children wish to add touches to their paintings. With a pencil that has been tied to the easel each artist writes his or her own name on a small dry area.

You will enjoy painless easel painting as much as the children.

If there are no floor easels available, you can make or buy cardboard easels that can be used on the tables or desks.

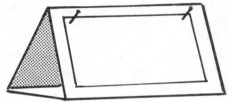

A homemade cardboard easel can be made from heavy corrugated cardboard. Fold and tape the cardboard into a triangle. Thumbtacks or straight pins will hold the paper on.

A shoebox or egg carton can hold paint. Have brushes and a can for water. Cover the desk or table with newspaper or oilcloth. A table near the sink could hold several cardboard easels and the painting supplies.

Seat Painting

Also allow the children to paint at their desks. Not everyone can work at an easel at the same time. Each child should keep his own desk cover, water can and painting shirt. Keep paint, brushes and paper available. Have a supply of plastic egg

Planning Painless Painting

cartons to hold small amounts of paint. Divide the twelve-section cartons into parts with a paper cutter. Watercolor and tempera cake sets are ideal for seat painting. Each child cleans up for himself. Again, provide a place for drying his work and storing it.

Floor Painting

There is no better place for many children to do large painting at the same time than a newspaper-covered floor. Use egg cartons or watercolor sets to hold the paint and orange juice cans for water. Adapt the kind of paper used to the job. Manila is good for individual watercolor or tempera paintings and roll paper in white or colors is best for scenery or group painting. There is no dripping and little spillage in floor painting. Organize aisles for walking. Have rags handy for emergencies. Extra egg cartons can be used to mix new colors.

If the weather is nice, paint outdoors on the blacktop and use a hose for cleanup. Remember to use stones to weigh down the paper. Pour liquid paint from squeeze containers into the egg cartons and distribute them after each child is settled in his place. Refill paint rather than pour large amounts that may be wasted.

It is possible to actually paint designs or pictures on old floors with acrylic paint. Get permission before beginning. This is permanent so preplan the design. Be sure to wash the floor first and then paint small sections at a time. Don't permit a child to paint himself into a corner. Polyurethane varnish should be used as a sealer when the work is dry.

Murals

What is a stimulating way to have the class practice working together? Even young children can set a common goal:

Organize groups and thoughts
Make decisions
Carry out their ideas
End up with a usable finished product

Toward the middle of the school year when you know the children well and they are familiar with several art techniques, it is time to work on a mural or on several at one time. Careful planning is important to avoid chaotic results.

Choose worthwhile topics. Let the mural be an outgrowth of a field trip, or a language arts or social studies unit. Show slides or pictures of colorful, emotionally moving murals done by the Mexican artists Diego Rivera and Orozco. Get pictorial representations of Indian kiva design murals. Show the current "Art by the People" murals in subway underpasses or on old buildings and walls. Explain that murals are large, even huge pieces of art expressing ideas. Stress that in a mural the background should be part of the total design. If the main objects are too small, there will be too much uninteresting open space to fill up.

A filmstrip and record combination by Alton S. Tobey in the series *Artists At Work*, distributed by Warren Schloat, exposes the class to resource techniques used by this professional muralist. After viewing the filmstrip, verbally connect profes-

Planning Painless Painting

sional approaches to gathering information and discuss actual methods of drawing and painting that can be used in a school situation. Insist on careful and accurate research from numerous sources rather than one. Have the boys and girls make many interpretive sketches using original drawings but employing factual ideas and actual colors and textures. Do not allow tracing or copying of any kind.

This is the opportunity to have each student utilize his own abilities. Who are the idea persons, the space planners, the organizers, designers, color specialists, detail persons, good workers, and setup and cleanup crew? Leaders and workers are all needed. Have the children divide into small, workable groups. Avoid personality clashes by stressing abilities. At times, an unpopular student or one who is not gifted academically may be one of the best artists. Let him excel where he can.

Procedure

Set some definite goals. What is the mural to show? What materials will be used? How much time is needed? How many artists work at a time, where can they work undisturbed, and how long are the working periods? What are the cleanup rules? Aim to have the mural finished by the end of the unit.

Choose the materials for the mural according to the need for permanency and how and where it will be placed when it is finished. Fired ceramic clay or acrylic paint directly applied to a wall that has been presized or painted with gesso are even suitable for outdoors. Plywood, masonite or cardboard covered with gesso and then painted can be hung in halls, libraries or other indoor locations. Hooked rug murals are also a permanent indoor decoration. Kraft or butcher roll paper should be used for play scenery, large poster murals, health, conservation or ecology campaign murals or other temporary uses. It is poor planning and poor economy to put months or even weeks of effort and work into something flimsy or easily ripped. If the children enjoy group work, they can make many different murals throughout the school year and choose when they will make one that is permanent.

After researching and making many drawings choose the best work. Plan how it will fit together as a whole. Have the children transfer the sketches to the background with an opaque projector. If that is not feasible, let them draw with chalk so that any mistakes can be wiped off with a damp cloth. Then trace it with pencil before color is applied. Overlapping of drawings is desirable.

The most important ideas should be largest and more prominent. Eliminate useless details. A mural is seen from a distance. Small or lightly drawn sections will not be seen. Large, clear forms show up best. Details and textures should be added last. Deciding on a color scheme before the work begins will help unify the project. Some flowing lines used as part of the background can also be used to unify the whole. Each section must work together as a unit to express the main idea. Fill up any empty spaces with texture or color.

Chalk on buttermilk or wet polymer as a binder, Craypas, tempera, collage, markers, fabric and mixed media are other good materials for mural work. Plenty of rags, newspaper, coffee cans and egg containers should be available. Have the group work on floors, walls, bulletin boards, table tops, in halls or any other areas where they and the materials will not block paths or entryways.

Decide when and how long each group will work. Pick a date when the work must be completed. Give the group large blocks of undisturbed working time so that the mural can be completed while the enthusiasm is still there.

It is hard to find an art experience that gives a greater sense of satisfaction than a well-executed mural.

Planning Painless Painting

Outdoor Painting and Sketching

There are many school days when it is nicer to be outdoors than inside. Consider outdoor art lessons whenever the weather permits. The problem of what to paint or draw is quickly solved outdoors. In fact, children must be taught to select what to draw or paint from all the things there are to see outside. A small cardboard frame held up to look through will help each child choose the subject that interests him or her.

Weather conditions are a consideration when planning the lesson and the medium to use. A calm day is best for using big sheets of drawing paper or making a large mural. A humid day will affect drying time so choose a bright, sunny day for your painting lesson.

Save large pieces of corrugated cardboard from boxes and get some big clips so that each child has a sturdy work surface. Clip several sheets of newsprint to the drawing board and have each child equipped with soft pencils, erasers, charcoal, crayons or chalk.

Paint that won't tip over and spill is best for outdoor use. Try using the new dry tempera cakes or watercolor sets. Each child will need a water can, a paint rag, a smock and manila paper.

Have the children save their quick outdoor sketches for a later painting lesson. Outdoor subject matter is unlimited (people, cars, trucks, buildings, nature and animals), so capture them on paper. Take time to study a leaf, the bark of a tree, or an ant climbing on a blade of grass.

Murals can be done outdoors if the day is calm and dry. Tear long sheets of butcher paper from a roll and attach these at the top and bottom to the outside of the building with strong masking tape. The paper can also be laid on a concrete or blacktop area and held in place with rocks. Organize the subject matter far ahead of time. Chalk and charcoal can be used on murals if permanency is not necessary. Use paint if the mural is to be lasting. Again the dry tempera blocks are easy to use. If you

Planning Painless Painting

don't have these, pour tempera paint into egg carton sections. Coffee cans of water and another container for brushes simplify cleanup. Take a large trash can outdoors with a plastic bag inside. When the painting is completed, throw the egg cartons inside and deposit the brushes in the cans of water. After soaking them, pour off the dirty water, wash the brushes indoors and store them heads up. The mural will dry quickly and can be taken inside for display. Chalk or charcoal work should be fixed outdoors (hair spray is a good fixative).

Check the recess schedule for the other grades so that your art lesson will be undisturbed. Stay out of wind paths and areas with bicycles, tanbark, or pebbles, which are distracting. A semishaded area away from school windows and doors is ideal. Wear a watch. Have all the children work in one area and have them all come together at a prearranged signal. Outdoor art is so much fun and so versatile you will want to plan several lessons when the weather is nice.

Cleanup Tips

Use this as a quick checklist:

Floors:

1. Wipe up spills on plastic floor covers.
2. Throw away old newspapers and replace with new ones for the next lesson.
3. Keep wet media and water near the sink so children do not walk across the room with wet paintings, brushes, and water cans.

Paints:

1. Have the cleanup crew wipe off the top of each jar and lid. Add a bit of "Vaseline" Petroleum Jelly to the jar edge before closing it.
2. When using semimoist watercolor or tempera, wipe off each cake of paint with a dry towel.

Brushes:

1. Wash each one thoroughly in water or soap or clean in solvent if necessary.
2. Store the brushes in a coffee can with heads up.
3. Wash the handles of the brushes.

Painting shirts:

1. Keep them in one place.
2. Wash them every so often.
3. Also wash paint rags when necessary.

Storage:

1. Try to store liquid paint *where it is cool*. At the end of the year, or at vacation time, recheck all paint containers for proper closure. This will make the next lesson easier.

Watercolor sets:

1. Be sure colors are clean and dry.
2. Keep a brush in each box.
3. Have a large, plastic tray to hold the boxes (a cardboard box works well, too).

Tempera cakes:

1. Have each color clean and dry.
2. Stack to store. Plastic trays or boxes keep these all together.
3. If they are to be stored for more than a few days, allow the paint to dry completely before storing.

Tempera:

1. Arrange extra jars on a shelf in colors. Large sizes are put in back of smaller ones.
2. Use old paint first. Open only one jar of each color.
3. Be sure lids are on straight and are tightened so the paint does not dry out.
4. Pour small amounts of paint into one jar so your storage area is not cluttered. Dabs of paint dry out quicker than large amounts. If a lid is spoiled or lost, make a temporary one from plastic wrap or tinfoil. Use a rubber band to secure.
5. If tempera paint is beginning to dry out but is soft to the touch, poke holes into it and fill the jar with water and close tightly. When you are ready to use it, stir the paint thoroughly so it is smooth and thick. The new plastic squeeze dispensers alleviate many of these storage problems.

Finger paint:

1. Store in color groups.
2. Make sure caps are put on securely.
3. Add water if they are too dry. Finger paint should be the consistency of soft pudding.
4. Try to store in a cool place.

Do not buy metal pans or small metal palettes. They rust and stick together when stacked and are simply additional items to clean. Plastic margarine containers and egg cartons are just as good, cost nothing and can be thrown away when necessary.

7 Artistic Adventures Open New Horizons: Putting Creativity to Use

What are we to do with our leisure time? How can we develop and enrich our lives? Each of us needs ways to express ourselves. The arts are the most satisfying expressions for many. Children, too, need to be given many opportunities to experiment with art forms and be allowed to use their creativity. It is the teacher's job to show each child a broader view of the world, in art forms as well as in academic studies. Art should be part of daily life, not just something to do once in a while. Try to be free, be inventive and be generous with time and materials if you wish to encourage creativity.

Calligraphy

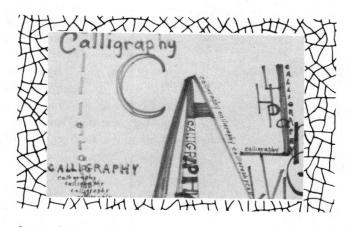

Calligraphy is the art of using letters, numerals and words in a creative manner. It provides a chance to communicate thoughts by combining written language and visual art. Line, form and color can be used in inventive and creative activities that involve calligraphy.

Getting Ready

Crayons or colored markers
9″ x 12″ white or manila paper

Let's Begin

"I want each of you to think about a word that is important, powerful, or has meaning for you. Each must have his or her own word. Let's be quiet for one minute while you think. You can close your eyes and cover your ears if it helps you think. When you have your word, tell me and then write it on the board. Now pretend the letters can be pulled and stretched. Who wants to come to the board and draw his word this way?

"When you get your paper, print or write your word as large, as small, or as tall as you can. Use thick and thin lines. What objects will tell about your word? Add some of these to your picture. Can you change a letter so it shows an object you want to use? Turn your paper around and fit the word into shapes you find but do not purposely draw shapes. Change the form of your paper by cutting the edges if it helps your design. When you have finished your written work, select colors that help express the word. What colors would make us feel sad, happy, sleepy, or angry?"

How Did It Work?

"What word has been used in a way that shows its importance? Do the symbols work with the letters to express the word? Where do you see color used in a way that depicts the meaning of the word? How will we use calligraphy again? Could you design a poster with powerful words and symbols using calligraphy?"

Artistic Adventures Open New Horizons

What Else?

Give each child a sheet of paper. Using crayon have each one print a numeral, a new letter from a handwriting lesson, a spelling or reading vocabulary word. Use another color crayon and go over and around the character or word many times. This eye and hand coordination reinforces the learning process. When this space on the paper has been filled, a watercolor wash around the written work adds color. One child told me her letter looked as if it were floating on air.

A good get-acquainted activity for the beginning of the school year uses each child's name. Precut 4½" x 6" pieces of manila paper. Each child prints the name so that the letters fill the space. Color all the shapes within and around each letter. Put the name designs on a bulletin board captioned "Here We Are" or "Names Are New."

Numeral calligraphy is attractive for a math exhibit. Precut 5" x 5" squares of manila paper. With a crayon, begin with one number large enough to almost fill the paper. Turn it and add more numerals, allowing the numbers to touch and overlap. Color around and in the shapes.

It is a challenge for older children to make designs using their signatures or spelling or vocabulary words as a starting point. The letters are cut from construction paper in all sizes, shapes and colors. The children can distort them to create interesting shapes. Glue them on another sheet of construction paper in a jumbled, tumbled manner to form a design. A freeform shape is cut around the edge. It is fun to find the hidden words.

Think of the name of an animal, fish, bird or reptile. Using the letters of the word in order, distort and exaggerate them any way necessary to create a picture of the word.

Design and crayon or paint a notebook or reading folder with names or initials.

Write and illustrate stories or poems. Illuminate the first letter of each line of a poem.

Draw large illustrations. Fit written areas into the illustration instead of at the bottom or side of the page.

Calligraphy can be used as an idea for stitchery. Use rug yarn and heavy cardboard. Write a word or name on the cardboard. Glue yarn on the letters and fill in the areas inside and around the word until the cardboard is covered. This is a good activity for learning disability groups.

Create posters and pictures using calligraphy as a functional part of the picture.

Mixed Media

A good way to assess your art program is to see how well the methods and skills you have taught are put to use. Mixing media is an artist's way of using his knowledge. If you want a certain effect, the best way to get it is to use several techniques in one piece of art work. Let the children discover new ways to use mixed media. You may be surprised at the results. Have the rest of the class see if they can tell which methods were used. Encourage this experimental approach.

At the end of the lessons in chapters 3, 4, 5, 7 and 8 there are suggestions for using mixed media.

    Collage
        Tissue and marker
        Marker or crayon and construction paper
        Mixed-media collage
        Acrylics on collage
        Mural collage
        Texture—fabric, wallpaper, wood, cardboard
        Scrap collage
        Wood and stain
    Watercolor and crayon resists
    Watercolor and marker

Artistic Adventures Open New Horizons

Watercolor and tempera
Chalk and polymer
Chalk on wet burlap
Chalk and polymer on paper towels
Finger paintings and cut paper
Finger paintings and marker
Finger paintings and tempera
Finger paint over crayon
Rubbings—crayon and watercolor resist
Marker over acrylics
Marker and tempera or watercolor
Marker on papier-mâché
Candle wax and watercolor or ink resist
Craypas and watercolor
Dry powdered tempera sprinkled on wet media
Tempera on polymer
Acrylics with cut paper or papier-mâché relief

From Drawing and Painting to Stitchery

This is an ancient art form that uses colored threads, fabrics and sometimes needles to depict an idea or merely to decorate with line, shape and color. The transition from drawing and using color to stitchery is creative when it is approached with an inventive attitude. Teach the term "stitchery" to the children. This art form appeals as much to boys as to girls if introduced properly.

Children should be encouraged to be free and creative in their approach. Avoid the coloring book method of filling in a pattern on fabric or drawing a picture to fill in. Stitchery will enhance a drawing or design as well as decorate fabrics and make toys and banners. Children learn to draw with their needle and yarn, invent their own stitches and make their own stitchery pictures and designs. Do not permit commercial patterns purchased in a store to be used. When the craftsman is the designer, the greatest satisfaction results.

Allow the children to choose their own colors, textures and stitches. When introducing stitchery to children be sure they are going to be successful. Plan the first project to be almost "too easy" for your group and let them expand. Never stop a child who can learn many stitches. There are so many combinations that can be made from the basic stitches that no two children should have identical results.

Getting Ready

Needles
Yarn

Crayons on construction paper

Markers on construction paper

Mural collage

Tempera and string painting

Tissue and marker collage

Artistic Adventures Open New Horizons

Polymer and tempera

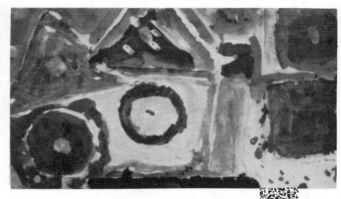

Collage and watercolor

Marker and watercolor

Texture collage

Chalk and marker

A piece of heavy manila paper with a simple line design drawn on it with
crayon—be sure there are straight lines and curved lines.
Stitchery books (see chapter 13)
Opaque projector

Let's Begin

"Who knows what stitchery is? Did you realize that you do not always have to
make a useful piece with stitchery? The books I have will show you some creative
stitchery by men and women who have created something fascinating with yarns and
threads. (Show five or six pictures or a piece of your own original work.) These people
create their own designs that do not look like any others.

"We will learn to thread a needle if you do not know how to do this. Then we
will do the two easiest stitches. Everyone will have a helper. (This lesson is a good
one in which to use aides, mothers, older children or other volunteers.)

"The running stitch begins by pushing the needle through the paper at the
end of a line you've drawn. The needle goes through the paper to the back again a
short distance away from the first stitch. The stitches you make should be even in
length with a short space between each one. What happens if you pull the thread too
tightly? (For kindergarten, young or inexperienced students, have the child use the
needle to make holes on the lines in the paper at intervals before they stitch. Then
even when the needle is in the back of the paper he will be able to see where to put
the next stitch.)

"Now we'll try some long and some short stitches. These are called straight
stitches and can be any size or go in any direction. Try some very long stitches. Keep
the thread loose when we work with cloth or it will be all puckered. Make very short
stitches. What could you use these for? How do straight stitches look when they
overlap? Stitch over all the lines on your paper. Change color when you wish and see
if you can invent some stitches." (This lesson may be presented in three parts
—showing stitchery pictures, threading a needle, and drawing the picture. Next
introduce the running stitch, and finally teach the straight stitch.)

  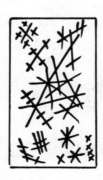

Artistic Adventures Open New Horizons

How Did It Work?

Mount the stitchery work on colored construction paper. Put the examples on a bulletin board. After a few days have an evaluation. "Did you enjoy stitchery?" "If you had problems, can you think of ways to improve next time?" "Which stitchery pictures have the most interesting use of stitches, the best colors, or look as if you can see deep into the stitches?"

What Else?

Try Other Stitches	Possible Grade Level
Running stitch	Kindergarten, first
Straight stitch	Kindergarten, first
Cross stitch	First, second
Back stitch	Second, third
Outline stitch	Second, third
Blanket stitch	Third
Couching	Second, third
Satin stitch	Third, fourth

Consider other materials:

Fabrics—Loosely woven such as burlap, heavy cotton or open-weave woolen fabrics, Styrofoam trays, paper.

Thread—Almost anything! String, yarn, threads, both cotton and metallic, cord, ribbon, grasses, threads pulled from burlap.

Needles—Very large-eyed, blunt-end, plastic or metal. Suggestions for needle substitutes are given in chapter 12.

Special effects—Beads, buttons, wire, rickrack, suede, leather, oilcloth, net, lace, mesh, onion bags, etc.

Projects to try:

The two beginning stitches are interesting when used on headbands, belts, or bookmarks.

Banners: "Crayon a design or a picture on burlap. Outline and accent the drawing with glued yarn or by using the basic stitches combine pieces of fabric and stitches into an appliqué. Sort the materials you have collected into the various color groupings. Notice the textures within each group. Are some rough, smooth, shiny and others dull or bright? Do you find different shades in each color group? Combine contrasting textures and shapes in various shades of a color into a pleasing design. Arrange them on a background and glue them into place. Add stitches that will fasten the pieces to the background and add detail to the design pattern. Combining fabric and stitches to a background in this way is called 'appliqué.'

"Make a design using many variations of one stitch. Combine yarns of different colors, textures and thicknesses. Vary the length of stitches, or arrange rows of stitches in stripes. In what other ways can you vary the stitch? By overlapping or placing the straight stitches so close together you see only the thread and color and not the fabric underneath.

"Stitch a picture using freehand stitchery as line. Enrich the line pattern with textural stitches and accent important areas sparingly with trimming materials such as sequins, buttons, braids, laces, beads or any other materials."

Encourage creative attitudes. Ask:

Who has selected shapes, colors and textures of materials in a new way?
Are the stitchery projects useful or decorative? If a piece is to be used, is it durable enough to meet its purpose?
Is the color selection closely related or one of contrasts?
Are shapes and colors repeated and do the lines flow through the design?
Is there diversity in shape, size and color so the design will be harmonious yet have variety?
Is there excellence in craftsmanship in accord with individual ability?

Weaving

Ways to weave are as varied and creative as any other form of stitchery. Color and shape are important in weaving as well as inventive use of threads, found and natural materials.

What weaving experience has each child had? If you find there are many who do not know how to weave, or if yours is a young group, then begin with paper weaving. When you introduce the lesson teach the basic weaving terms.

Weaving—The interlacing of threads to
form a weblike fabric.

Artistic Adventures Open New Horizons

Loom—A frame to hold threads in place, under tension, so that threads may be woven in the opposite direction.

Warp thread—The thread that is placed on the loom first, into which the cross threads are woven.

Filler thread—The thread that is woven into the warp thread. (Technically this is called the weft or woof.)

Getting Ready

Two different colors of 12″ x 18″ construction paper
Scissors
Pencil and crayon
Ruler
Glue

Let's Begin

"Do you know how fabric is made? Have you ever done weaving? We will learn how to weave on a paper loom. Can anyone tell me what the word 'loom' means?

"Take one color of paper. With a pencil measure in one inch, making dots along all four sides. Using your ruler connect the dots to form a frame.

"Fold the paper in half with the pencil lines showing and the fold on top.

"Watch me as I draw four or five crayon lines from the fold to the pencil line on the bottom. Keep wide spaces between the lines. Cut along the crayon lines. Make sure the paper is still closed. Unfold your paper and look at it. The paper frame is the loom and the wide strips we cut are now the warp. (Try to have a picture of a real frame loom that is warped to show the children the similarities.)

"You need some paper strips to weave into the warp. These are called the fillers. With the other color, cut strips about an inch wide. (These can be precut on the paper cutter for very young children.)

"The filler will be laced in and out (or over and under) the warp strips. Watch me. The first filler strip goes in (or under) then out until you've woven each warp strip. The second filler goes out (or over), then in, as we did the first strip. The third filler will be woven like the first one and so on. This type of weave is called 'tabby.' Fill the warp as full of strips as you can so that the paper loom is strong again. You may glue the loose ends along the edges."

How Did It Work?

Has everyone mastered the weaving technique? Are there many varied designs? Who has thought of something different to do with the paper looms?

What Else?

More complicated patterns may be cut or torn into the paper looms. Wavy or zigzag strips for fillers create a new look. Try using straight and fancy strips together as well as more than two colors.

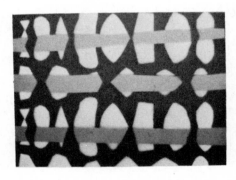

Artistic Adventures Open New Horizons

Try weaving for special effects on a realistic shape.

Handweaving is done in so many ways that you can have several projects during the year. Here are some ways to weave.

Styrofoam Tray Weaving—Use the white meat trays found in many stores. Cut out and remove the center of the tray carefully. Punch holes ½" from the edge to string the warp. There must be an odd number of holes around the edge of the tray. Begin weaving in the center. Vary the thickness and kinds of thread. The weaving should be done very loosely to create textural interest. The finished piece will have a web effect.

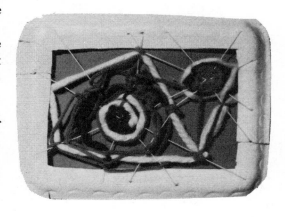

Cardboard Weaving—You will need corrugated cardboard or very strong scrap cardboard. Measure and cut slits every ½" at the top and bottom. Tie a knot and slip the thread in slit #1, go up to #2. Go across the back to slit #3, down over the front to #4, across the back to notch #5, and so on. To end the warping tie a know in #28. Now begin weaving back and forth. When you change colors or come to the end of a piece of yarn do not tie the end. Leave ends loose and weave them in later. Vary the thickness and color of yarn for interest.

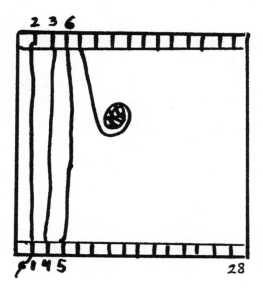

Artistic Adventures Open New Horizons

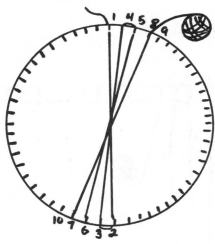

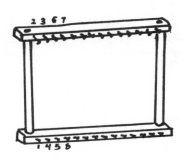

For young children, to avoid pulling too tightly at the sides, precut the filler yarn into pieces five inches wider than the loom. Let these ends hang as fringe. Be sure to pack the filler tightly. When the weaving is done, slip the warp threads off the cardboard. Surprisingly enough it does not unravel. Several pieces of weaving may be sewn together for a wall hanging. Lace a stick or dowel rod through the top. Two sections may be sewn together at the sides and bottom to create a pouch. Older children may want to create geometric or freeform shapes to weave on.

Weaving in the Round—Paper plates, cardboard, or plastic lids are used as looms for the warping. Cut slits in the edge as for cardboard weaving. Use an odd number of slits. The warp is strung as shown. Begin weaving in the center, pulling the yarn tight to start. As the space between the warp threads gets wider, loosen the tension of the filler yarn. The yarn can remain on the loom for a wall hanging or be removed if you wish.

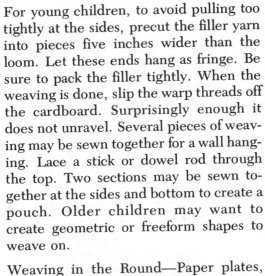

Wood Frame Weaving—Ask the clerks in a notion department to save the frames their trims and lace are on. They are usually made of wood and can be made into perfect looms. Have the children measure, mark and pound nails into the flat edges at ½" intervals. Now warp the loom as in cardboard weaving and you are ready to begin.

Artistic Adventures Open New Horizons

Slip the warp threads off the nails to remove the finished piece.

Stick Weaving—These looms must be hung on a knob, taped to the desk, or in nice weather tied to a fence outdoors. If hung, the weight of the bottom stick will keep the warp taut. The warp threads are simply tied on the sticks, and the filler threads woven back and forth. If stick looms are taped to the desk, the tape holds the sticks in place so that weaving may be done.

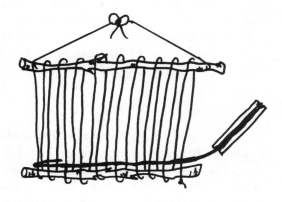

Older children can develop patterns in weaving by using several colors of filler or weft thread. Cardboard weaving adapts to patterns readily. Here are a few simple patterns. Encourage the children to develop their own patterns.

Color A—Two rows
Color B—Four rows   or
Color A—Two rows

Color A—One row
Color B—One row
(Repeat this three times)
Color B—One row
Color A—One row
(Repeat this three times)

When using two colors do not cut the thread when you change colors. Carry the color not used along the edge of the work until it is needed.

Slit Weaving—This type of weave creates open spaces or separate panels between the warp threads.

Encourage the children to think of ways to make rectangular weaving pieces useful as well as decorative. Small rugs can be made by sewing pieces together.

Handweaving should have great textural interest. Use a variety of threads and weave freely in a loose manner, unless the weaving is to be used, such as a bag. The colors will be as varied as you care to make them. Young children lose patience with yarn that is too thin. Collect many varieties of yarn. Color and thickness of yarn are unlimited. Keep straws, sticks, grasses and weeds in a box. Weaving with these adds textural interest. Go for a walk in the fall and see how many dried materials you can find. Cornhusks and dried corn silk are wonderful fillers to use.

Rug Punching

The soft, shaggy effect of rug punching is more adaptable to bold, geometric or freeform shapes than to intricate line detail. Take the time to work out an original, cut-paper design of shapes with a simple color scheme. Transfer this design to the burlap backing for your rug. This is a project that will take weeks to complete but each child can work in free time at his or her own pace. A child with little patience or a slow worker should plan a small piece.

Getting Ready

A previously executed design
Various colors of cotton rug yarn or four-ply knitting worsted
Rug punch needles (Columbia Minerva or Boye with wooden handles are best. Be sure there is an adjustment on the needle for stitch length.)
Hammers and rug tacks
Heavy-duty stapler and staples
A frame—a handmade one, a commercial adjustable rug frame, an old TV table (legs only) or picture frame (see page 178)
Burlap—unbleached preferably

Let's Begin

First session—"Do you enjoy rubbing your hand over a soft carpet? Have you ever seen a colorful, shaggy carpet hung on a wall? We will use designs you've just made for our rugs. You have your frames ready and your rug punch needles. We will tack the burlap to the frame just this way. This will be our practice piece when we begin the rug punching. Do one edge first. Work with a partner. Your helper will hold the burlap taut while you tack it. Now tack the opposite edge, this keeps the burlap tight on the frame. Now do the other sides. Draw your design on the back of the burlap with a marker just as we've worked it out." (An opaque projector can be used.)

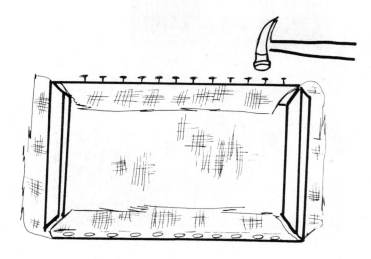

Second session—"Today we will learn to thread the rug needles and practice rug punching on our demonstration piece. Each child is ready to begin at a different time. It doesn't take long to learn. The back should have small, even stitches and the front will have loops."

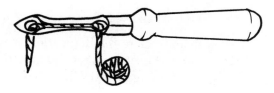

NOTE: The needles you buy, or that the children bring, will have different ways to adjust stitch length, but all are threaded in this way. The yarn must run through the needle easily.

"After you can thread a rug needle, select a color of yarn and roll it into a small ball. Put one end through the first hole. Now pull it down to the second hole in the needle and pull it through leaving a short end, at least two inches.

"Adjust your stitch length, a medium one is best to begin. Do not use the stitch adjuster for long loops. Work with the design facing you. Hold the needle with the grooved side upward. Punch through the burlap and draw the needle back through the hole. Keep the point of the needle close to the fabric and push down again very close to the first stitch. Keep punching for several rows. Turn the frame over to see if your stitches are even.

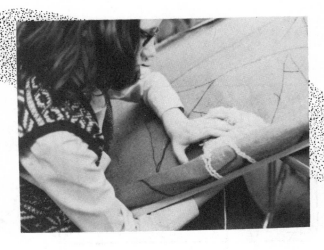

"When you wish, change the yarn color and the length of your stitch. Cut off the end of the yarn in the back and leave it there. Do not knot or tie the yarn. Begin again and continue until your design is complete. Don't be afraid to rip out poor work—craftsmen aim for perfection. When the rug is complete, paint or spray a rubberized rug base on the back to hold the stitches."

How Did It Work?

Have the children learned to appreciate the dedication of craftsmen? Do they enjoy their own designs? Have they varied the stitch length to create a high-low effect in the pile? Do the colors blend and contrast effectively?

What Else?

Make a picture-type design using bold, colorful shapes and a few lines. Let the picture fill nearly the entire area.

Mixed media—Add rug punching to appliqué and stitchery pieces for special effects.

Design a rug punching for a group of children to make as a permanent wall hanging for the school.

Artistic Adventures Open New Horizons

8

New Media
with Exciting Results

What is it going to look like? Excitement prevails as tie-dyed articles are untied. Can this crumpled, dripping waxed cloth be beautiful? Yes, and children enjoy trying the methods and media that are not completely predictable. Tie-dye, batik and using stain produce successful results and anyone can learn how to work with them.

Abstract and freeform designs can be put to use. Learn how to batik using cut-paper designs or drawings done in another lesson.

Control of an X-acto knife is a useful skill. Inventiveness is encouraged when the student experiments with shapes cut with a knife and other media.

Tie-dye—A New Twist

What is more fun than making something beautiful and being able to wear it too?

The class has already learned how colors mix to form new shades and tints. The children know that light colors should be used first, the darkest ones last and that mixing more than three colors together produces a brown tone. Review these facts with them. We are now ready for the dyeing.

Getting Ready

Smocks

Yellow, blue, red, and green liquid or powder permanent dye for fabrics (Liquid dye does not need hot water; powdered dye does, but it does not have to be boiling as directions indicate.)

A white tee shirt, pillowcase, pair of shorts, scarf or handkerchief

Small rubber bands

Sticks

Four buckets

Four coffee cans

Four brushes

Newspaper

Plastic bags

Let's Begin

If the weather is warm, work outdoors. If not, use plenty of newspapers to protect working surfaces.

"Now each of you will take about twenty rubber bands. Begin to gather one small part of your fabric at a time and then wind it as tightly as possible with the rubber band. Make some large bunches and some small ones."

Give the ground rules and check to see that the rubber bands are really tightly wound and that they have made *many* ties. Remind everyone that the colors will dry very much lighter, almost as pastel colors.

Demonstrate how to make tight bundles on a piece of white cloth.

Show a large bundle   and   small clumps   and   pushing a section
                                                                              down with a pencil.

   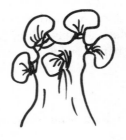   

Tie the cloth so many times that it no longer looks like a shirt, pillowcase, handkerchief or whatever you are dyeing.

Show pleating,   folding   and banding.

Immerse part of the tied cloth in one color and dip the rest in another. Squeeze the excess dye out before dipping in another color. Use a very dark dye solution in a coffee can and apply color with a brush to some folds and near the banding. Remove the rubber bands (which can be reused) and open the cloth. Answer questions now about how certain effects were created.

New Media with Exciting Results

Rit Dye offers a free booklet worth sending for. Write to: Dye-Craft Ideas, Box 307 Dept. GL-9, Coventry, Conn. 06238.

The children can hardly wait to begin.

"I will mix the colors into hot water in the buckets and stir them with a stick while you work. In front of each bucket will be a small amount of dark dye in a coffee can, which you can apply with the brush whenever you need a dark color. When you are ready, I'll check your banding and then you can start to dye."

How Did It Work?

When everyone has had a chance to tie and dye and all the rubber bands have been put into a box to dry, have the children spread their fabric on the grass or newspaper (indoors) so the others can admire the results. The oohs and ahs shouldn't surprise you but the designs will. This is an art lesson where even the least creative child may have an outstanding piece.

Each child may take his wet fabric home in a plastic bag. Some teachers prefer to have one or two children bring them all home for the group and put them into the dryer after soaking them in a vinegar and water bath to help set the dye.

What Else?

Plan to have the children wear their garments one day soon.

Make wall hangings or scarves another time for special gifts using the techniques the youngsters liked best or invented for themselves.

Dye a yard of plain fabric and make the material into a necktie for a gift.

Stain

How many boys and girls have ever polished shoes? Shoe polish in liquid or paste form is an excellent art medium.

Getting Ready

Permanent markers
Black, brown, red and blue shoe polish in liquid and/or paste form
Sandpaper
One piece of plywood for each child
Rags
Newspaper
Pro-Tek (DuPont)—the invisible glove
Soap

New Media with Exciting Results

"We are going to use our imaginations to create strange new sights. First, cover your desk. Look at your wood. As you sand it smooth, notice the ridges and special markings that make your piece unique or something special. Turn your wood around and then over to the other side. Which side has the best swirls and lines?"

Let's Begin

"We are going to emphasize the grain of the wood by rubbing shoe polish stain over the front and sides. Use the lighter color polish first in some areas. Now add a darker color polish for contrast. Wherever you want something to look mysterious or far away, rub with a darker color. What does it begin to look like? Rub the whole piece with a clean rag. Do you see some important places? Should parts be even darker? Would a marker make an important part stand out? Remember to use contrast, dark and light, thick and thin, negative and positive. Turn your wood around. Look at it from a distance. Can you see it from six feet away? Should certain parts be exaggerated? See what kind of a mood you can create."

How Did It Work?

"Which pieces show the best use of the shapes and swirls found in the wood? Why? Is there one that shows good use of contrast between darks and lights? Do you like the addition of the markers?"

What Else?

Go one step further by adding watercolor paint, string or scrap fabrics.

Try stain on Pariscraft, Sculptamold, ceramics, cardboard, burlap and plaster of Paris.

Crayon Batik—The Brush Off!

Batik is an art form in which areas of fabric are covered with hot, melted wax and then dipped in colored dyes. The wax in authentic batik protects each color

New Media with Exciting Results

as successive dyes are used. Heat is then used to remove the wax. Crayon batik, used in school, simplifies the procedure. Melted crayon is both the coloring agent and the wax. An iron is used to remove the wax. The results are beautiful and well worth the effort. Through the years children should have many experiences with crayon or candle resists using varied wet media such as watercolor, tempera, acrylic and dye. Crayon batik takes the resist techniques a step further.

Getting Ready

A small electric hot tray or electric skillet
An old metal muffin tin—6, 8, or 12 sections
Old brushes in varied widths, both soft and stiff bristles
Cotton swabs
Used broken crayons in many colors, which the children and you donate
    through the year
Melted paraffin
Pieces of previously washed white fabric (old pillowcases, sheets, unbleached
    muslin—no permanent press fabrics)
An iron
One package of Dylon cold dye or bottle of liquid dye in any dark color
Plastic bucket or can for dye
Piles of newspaper and paper towels
A large, flat table to hold the fabric, skillet, brushes and muffin tin with
    melted crayons and paraffin diluted half and half. Place it near an
    electrical outlet (for the electric skillet and iron). Try to push the table
    against the wall to eliminate the possibility of walking into the cords
    and spilling the melted crayons or dropping the iron.

Let's Begin

"Who remembers what happens when we paint over crayon or wax? Right! The wax resists the wet materials and we see an effect that we could not produce from crayons or paint alone. We will learn a new way to use this idea. It is called crayon batik. We are going to use melted crayons and wax on cloth and paint a design or picture with brushes or cotton swabs dipped in the hot crayon, which will color the fabric. When the material is covered with the melted colors and the wax is dry and hard, roll the fabric and squeeze it gently to crackle the wax. Be careful not to squeeze so hard that the wax chips off. Carefully unroll the cloth and lay it flat on the newspapers again. Take the wide, stiff brushes and paint the dye all over the cloth or dip it into a large pan. Apply it over all the waxed areas. Lay the cloth on fresh newspapers to dry.

"When the batik is dry the wax must be melted away. Plug in the iron on low heat. Place the material on a thick pad of newspaper with the crayon side up. Have a partner help you cover the design with paper towels. Begin ironing. The wax will melt onto the paper towel. Remove it and put another towel over the ironed area. Continue ironing, melting wax and using new towels until no more wax comes off. The colors from the crayon are now permanent and combined with the dye it provides an interesting cracked effect."

How Did It Work?

"How does crayon batik compare to crayon resist? Do you like the crackle effect and the dye bleeding into the crayon colors? Could we make something with our batik?"

What Else?

Make scarves, pillows or neckties with the fabrics.
Try a wall hanging or simple curtains with the batik.
Print over it—potato prints or string prints.
Design from nature—leaves, pods, flowers, plant life, trees
    Sea life—shells, starfish, coral, fish
    Fossils
    Microscopic forms—protozoa, amoeba
    Sun, moon, planets
    Animal life
    Birds

Perhaps the class will want to make a large, mural-type batik or wall hanging for the school.

More advanced students can make batik pieces for shirts, vests or skirts.

X-acto Knife Forms

Here is a skill that can be easily taught to a group of five or ten children at a time who in turn can help teach others in another session.

Many youngsters have already used knives in scouting or in building plane, rocket or ship models.

New Media with Exciting Results

Once anyone has mastery over an X-acto knife, he will see the advantages it has over scissors in cutting out newspaper or magazine articles, complicated forms for designs, and the inside of circular shapes without spoiling the outer forms.

Getting Ready

One X-acto handle and sharpened blade per child
The classified sections of Sunday newspapers
Newspaper or cardboard to use as a base

Let's Begin

"Do any of you know a way to cut out shapes without using scissors? Once you know how to use an X-acto knife you will like to work with it. We are going to hold the knife like a piece of chalk, not like a pencil.

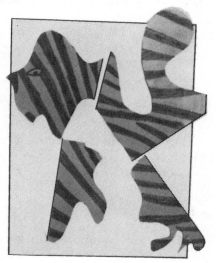

"Check to see that the blade is tight. Put the newspaper on your desk with the lines separating the want-ad columns running vertically. With a firm stroke pull the knife from the top of the page to the bottom trying to follow the lines. Don't worry if you aren't able to do it at first. Keep practicing. Try it twenty-five times or until you are satisfied with the results.

"Now see if you can make horizontal cuts. If you are right-handed, it may be easier to cut from left to right. If you are left-handed, cut from right to left. Do this twenty-five times. Next try to see if you can cut out a newspaper article. Cut out a number of articles including one from the center of a page. Try to cut out the center article keeping the rest of the page intact. Try to control the depth of your cut so that you go through only one layer of paper at a time.

"Turn the newspaper over to the side without cuts. We are going to make "S" shapes. Rotate and turn the handle of the knife so that it moves smoothly.

New Media with Exciting Results

Carefully practice this in the air until you get the feel of it. Hold it loosely and let the handle roll between your fingers. Now try to make the wiggle shapes on the newspaper. You will notice that if you rotate the blade slowly you will have wider curves but if you move the blade and handle slightly faster you will make smaller curves. Let the knife move smoothly. Make large arcs and small ones. Can you trace a curved shape made with a marker on the newspaper? Try to cut out the shape of a person's figure from one of the ads. Make sure you don't rip instead of cutting. Do it smoothly."

How Did It Work?

"Are you able to cut lines and curves using the knife? Are the cuts as clean as they should be or are they jagged and ripped? Can you cut any size or shape article from a newspaper or magazine?"

What Else?

With proper supervision let one or several children work at a newspaper-covered table using scrap paper or newspaper and practice making unusual shapes as they gain better control of the knife. Arrange the cut-out shapes on construction paper for collages. Glue them down. Use markers or paint to enhance the shapes.

Try calligraphy with a knife making newspaper letters or numbers. Be as free as you can. Exaggerate for an interesting effect.

When the skill of using an X-acto knife has been mastered, try cutting construction paper or wallpaper for a variety of textures and colors.

9 Tricks of the Trade

In every profession there are tricks that make things easier. Here are some to make your art program more workable.

Preparation Prevents Problems

Each of us has had the awful experience of starting to teach a lesson and suddenly realizing that we had not prepared ourselves or our materials sufficiently. Preparation prevents problems. To have well-organized lessons:

Know your class—Build on what the children already know. Utilize their strengths and weaknesses. Art skills develop like other skills.

Preplan—Know the skills and materials involved in the lesson and know why you are teaching it.

Materials—As you plan a lesson jot down everything you'll need. Get the supplies organized and ready to distribute well ahead of time. Open paint jars, check quantities and so on.

Work areas—Desks, tables and floors must be arranged so that the lessons go smoothly. Are there protective coverings? Can everyone see the demonstration? Do you need group work areas or individual places?

Drying areas—Prepare a spot out of the way of traffic for work to dry. Have plenty of newspaper to protect the surface of the drying area.

Storage areas—Constructions, stitchery or clay pieces need to be put on shelves where they can dry safely without being touched.

Assistants—Pretrain your helpers and arrange to have them available when needed.

Prior preparations avoid last-minute trips to the storage room or to find the custodian.

To avoid problems remember to:

Build on skills; have a sequential art program.

Avoid involved projects and holiday art.

Be sure each lesson is teacher-motivated, not teacher-executed.

Be sure your class has good working habits and knows cleanup procedures.

Cover work and drying areas so that cleanup is easy.

Do the right project at the right time. Remember, weather affects some art media.

Printmaking—Never print with ink on a damp, humid day. The ink takes longer to dry.

Plaster of Paris, Pariscraft—Work outside if possible, or over newspaper. Precut strips of Pariscraft to avoid dust. Moist weather slows the drying. Use a broom or vacuum cleaner to clean up, never a wet sponge or cloth.

Help Is Always Available

No one excels in everything so don't hesitate to seek help when you need it. Above all, don't avoid teaching art because you feel insecure. When you plan an art lesson help is always available.

Consult your art supervisor or art teacher. They are trained to help you. Once the lesson is planned, find and pretrain parents or volunteers to assist you in the classroom. Many times the adults are experts in the field and can actually teach the lesson while you assist.

Plan ahead and prepare idea books, scrapbooks, notebooks or card files of ideas and processes you have developed for your own use. Send for free literature (see chapter 12). Obtain films, filmstrips and slides to help you. Go to the local library and get how-to-do-it books. There are some excellent art magazines that are helpful listed in chapter 13.

Once you have tapped some of these sources you will discover others that may be even better.

Build on Skills

One of the nicest parts of starting a school year is seeing friends again and making new acquaintances. Your art program should work in the same way. The old friends are the media—crayon, chalk, watercolor and tempera painting. The new friends are fresh, innovative ways to use the media, plus the introduction of additional skills.

Your attitude is important in building skills. Let the children know that you hope they will all become experts in some area. Talk about artists and craftsmen and stress the fact that they work hard to become proficient, to profit from mistakes and constantly use their skills over and over, always seeking new ways to work. The filmstrips, *Famous Artists at Work*, mentioned in chapter 12, are good to use to inspire the children to work as artists do.

Be eager to share your abilities with the children. You are their closest source of inspiration.

Plan your art program as a sequential series of skills that you introduce and expand upon each year.

You should learn to gauge class abilities, so talk to last year's teacher. Ask her to help you find out what art experiences the children have had or ask the children to talk about art lessons they enjoy. You can have the boys and girls check a list of skills

Tricks of the Trade

they think they can do well, or have them indicate where help is needed. Find out their feelings about art. Do they enjoy it or feel uneasy about it? Let them know that many times a medium they have not liked before may be their favorite one this year, perhaps because they have grown up, can do it better now, or will learn something new about it. An open mind toward art will help you build on skills.

Know the Pitfalls

Certain things don't work. Know what they are in advance. Nothing replaces having tried the lesson by yourself.

Have you ever attempted to dry paintings on a damp day? Don't. Instead, paint on a clear day. Be sure you have enough drying space on the floor, on bulletin boards or on clotheslines.

If your plans include mural work throughout the year, get permission to attach cork strips to the walls so that the paper can be stapled or pinned on at the top and bottom and won't come loose.

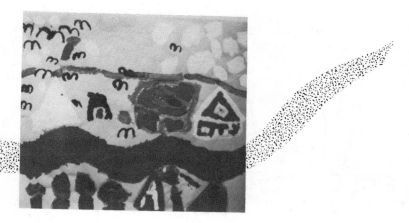

Do your picture displays fall off the windows? You may have unsuccessfully tried masking tape or cellophane tape on them. Some schools have a policy forbidding such tapes on the windows. Here's a good use for Metylan art paste, the art material that looks and feels like colorless gelatin but glues paper, fabric and cardboard to paper, fabrics, wood, Styrofoam and glass. Nothing is faster or easier to remove from windows. Use water to thin or remove it when necessary. It does not make a stiff residue on a desk or on fingers as white glue does.

When someone wants to enlarge a drawing and transfer the image to another surface, as for a mural, use the opaque projector. Another way is to have the drawing made on a transparency and use an overhead projector.

Have a pile of rags to wipe up sudden spills. Paper towels aren't a substitute in an emergency or for big jobs.

Organize your desk drawer to hold clips, pins, tacks, rubber bands, etc. by using wide-mouthed discarded paste jars. Enlist the custodian's help in salvaging these.

Avoid dried-out markers by having the students place them in large coffee cans with the covered end up. Keep extra caps in your drawer to instantly replace any that have been lost.

Keep a scrap box of unusual items. Stack larger pieces on a shelf. Train the class to look for and bring things all during the year. This saves writing notes for needed items at the last minute. Plan some lessons to use what you have rather than what you need.

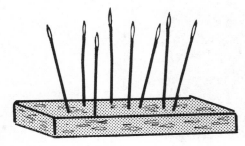

Use a sponge to hold needles rather than a box. They won't fall out or get lost. At a glance you can easily tell how many there are.

Transfer paint from old glass jars to plastic ones using a funnel. Relabel them. Even a kindergartener can learn to pour out his own paint.

Empty squeeze bottles from detergents or liquid margarine are handy paint or glue dispensers.

Simple Tools—
How to Use and Care for Them

Every teacher should have a supply of brushes, various knives, scissors and glue. Know which ones are needed for a particular job and how to care for them. This not only prolongs their lives but keeps them in usable condition at all times. The most valuable of all tools are our fingers and we can learn to use them more sensitively.

Tricks of the Trade

Brushes

Keep soft, pointed watercolor brushes and stiff easel brushes separate. Use coffee cans to store them with bristles *up*. Near the sink is a good place to keep them. Brushes must be properly cleaned at once after each use. Refer to the solvent chart in this chapter.

Scissors

Sharp-pointed scissors that cut well are the only ones to use. They are more expensive but the others do not do the job. If each child is required to bring his own, let the parents know what to buy. Scissors can be stored in many types of containers but the cheapest and simplest is a can in which the scissor points down and the handles stick out.

Use scissors only to cut, never to pry open lids or make holes in things. Use the proper tool for each job. It is sometimes necessary to walk around with scissors. Teach each child to hold the blades closed with the point toward the floor and to walk, not run. When it is handed to someone the student holds on to the closed blades and extends the handle to the other person. To sharpen scissors, make several slits in a piece of sandpaper. If the blades do not open easily, put some lubricating grease on the hinge.

Knives

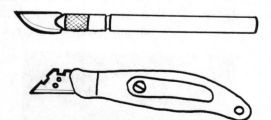

X-acto knives are used to cut paper and small areas where it is difficult to use scissors. A small group of upper-grade children can be given a lesson in using knives.

Some already do at home. Remember to keep the blades sharpened with a whetstone. A dull knife is a dangerous one.

Intricate shapes cut with an X-acto tool make wonderful designs. Whole pages or articles are easily cut from newspapers or magazines (see chapter 8). No child should use a knife without supervision or if he can't follow instructions. We all have to learn to use dangerous tools, but not all students are ready to start at the same time.

A Stanley knife, with its retractable blade, is indispensable for slicing up heavy cardboard boxes. This is not a community tool and should be used only by an adult or by one child at a time who can be trusted. The youngster must be under adult supervision and must first prove to the adult that he knows how to use the tool.

All knives are stored in a locked area. Each child is responsible for his or her tool and returns it directly to the teacher. A knife is not turned over to another person or left around after use. Set aside a quiet work area when someone is using a dangerous implement where you can watch and supervise if necessary.

Glue

Glue is annoying to get out of the container. Use one large jar and pour small amounts onto plastic lids for several people to share and use with fingers. It is easier to put more on the lid than pour some back.

Binney & Smith makes an excellent dispenser that does pour. Other companies have worked on improved package design, too, but this type of simple device works best for busy youngsters or teachers.

Fingers

The best tools are fingers. You always know where to find them. When ripping, tearing, gluing, texturizing or indenting, folding, fingerpainting or twisting, don't forget to try your fingers. Have a bar of soap and plenty of paper towels so everyone can wash glue, pencil, charcoal and paint off fingers easily.

Tricks of the Trade

Know Your Solvents

Make two copies of this solvent chart and tape one to the inside of your closet door at home and one at school. Even if you need it only once, you will be glad to have it where you can find it.

SOLVENT CHART

ART MATERIAL	SOLVENT
Oil-based stains Enamel Varnish	Turpentine or mineral spirits, followed by soap and water.
India ink—waterproof	Water with a few drops of ammonia.
India ink—water soluble	Water.
Printer's ink	Kerosene or turpentine.
Shellac	Alcohol, followed by soap and water
Oil paint	Turpentine.
Lacquer	Lacquer thinner.
Acrylic paint	Water while still wet. Isopropyl (drugstore) alcohol when dry.
Crayon	Turpoline, paint thinner or turpentine.
Wax	Chip or scrape off excess, then iron between absorbent paper.

**How to Clean Up Your Closets
and Have a Great Art Lesson
at the Same Time**

By the end of the school year the boys and girls have tried so many different art ideas, why not have a choice of media art lesson?

Set out a selection of materials and let the children choose. Perhaps the child who was absent when the class did stitchery or chalk or watercolor would like to do it now. What about the boy who never quite finished when everyone else did? He can do it now. Then there is the youngster who only likes to draw when you have another lesson planned. This is the time when he can do it. The group of children who always wanted to work together but never were on the same committee might work on a mural, diorama or 3D project. Someone who had no confidence to try the new media you introduced earlier may wish to try it before school is out.

Here's how to plan:

1. Set aside a large, cleared area.
2. Cover it with newspaper to facilitate cleanup.
3. Put out:
    watercolors
    water cans
    poster paint
    clay
    glue
    leftover scrap materials (that you don't want to save for next year)
    construction paper—use every conceivable size
    wire and pliers
    drawing paper
    cardboard
    newsprint
    burlap
    yarn
    tissue paper scraps
    Styrofoam
    rags and sponges
    whatever else you can think of
4. Each child signs up (in the upper grades) or chooses material and sets to work. Everyone may experiment but not waste.
5. Leave time for an exhibit or have the children make a bulletin board.
6. Let each child evaluate his or her own work.

You may decide to have another choose-your-own-medium lesson. This is usually very popular with students and teachers, too.

10   All Day Counts: Creative Action Involves the Whole School Day

Art Is Everywhere

Who knows where to find all the sounds and reflections of beauty? Let's not look for them only in the art room or art corner. Art is everywhere:

A book—a picture
A song—a sound
A poem—a thought

These are art.

A landscape scene, one single leaf, a dance or even a step are forms of art as well. What about a movement or an interpretation; a natural texture or even an arrangement of objects? Allow your senses to help you and the children experience beauty. Look for opportunities to integrate art into your school program in a natural way rather than an artificially segregated forty-minute art period each week. Encourage the class to become aware of current cultural exhibits, good music or books and special T.V. programs. Don't expect creativity in an art lesson if you suppress individual ideas during the rest of the school day. Reward the self-motivated student who creates his own learning opportunities. Your total teaching program must generate a feeling of enthusiasm and innovation so each child will be eager to learn more by himself. Learning just begins in the classroom.

Art and Language Arts

What is the most creative way to use the language skills we possess? Why not write a book and illustrate it? In a book we express our own ideas and thoughts, put knowledge to use and communicate with others. Any child who knows the alphabet can write a book. Have beginning readers make an illustrated alphabet book. Older children have a wealth of things to write about, a funny person, an animal, an event, a trip, the zoo, a spooky story or a sad happening. Just give them the chance. After their thoughts are down on paper,. they may need help with organization. *Do not rewrite or criticize their material.*

Gwen

Gwen Rodrick
In the oldn days.
Thar wus a woter
sprikelr. All of the
childinfolode the woter—

Children's books are most appealing printed or written in their own handwriting. Boys and girls can use markers to make handsome illustrations if the paper is heavy enough so the marker ink does not bleed through to the other side. Pictures can be done on drawing paper and cut and pasted in an appropriate spot. Crayon pictures also are attractive. The illustrations must be the child's own ideas and work.

Covers and Binding

Covers are easy. Have two pieces of construction paper with holes punched in three places. Lace with yarn and tie. Cardboard or tagboard, which are more durable, can be used in the same way.

The best way to cover a book is to stitch and bind it. Use:

8″ x 10″ paper*—enough for all the written and illustrated material. Try white drawing paper, ditto or mimeograph paper and notebook paper with pictures pasted on.

Cardboard—9″ x 12″ or 12″ x 20″*

Covering for cardboard—12″ x 14″*—fabric, burlap, wallpaper or finger paintings can be used.

Place the cardboard on paper or fabric to be used for a cover. Score the center of the cardboard with the point of a scissors using a ruler as a guide.

Brush glue on the opposite side of the cardboard, completely covering the surface. *Carefully* place the cardboard in the center of the covering material and rub from the center out to the edge. This removes all the bubbles. Put this under pressure (heavy books or an unheated dry mount press) until the glue is dry.

*All sizes can be larger or smaller if different-sized books are made.

Creative Action Involves the Whole School Day

Fold fabric or paper cover over the four corners of cardboard. Cut off shaded areas.

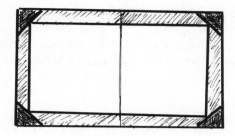

Brush glue on the remaining edges of the book covering. Fold over on the cardboard and hold until the glue sticks.

Now glue a sheet of paper (8″ x 10″) over the fabric and cardboard so a small edge of covering remains and the cardboard is covered.

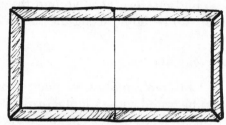

Fold the cover toward you; the scored line will be your fold line. Fold as many 8″ x 10″ pages as needed in half. With a needle or pointed scissors put at least six holes so the needle and thread can go through all the paper and the cover. These must be lined up evenly. An adult should help with this. Tie a large knot in the end of the cord and thread a large-eyed blunt needle.

Leave three or four inches of cord to tie when stitching is completed. Use the running stitch and then go back, filling in spaces between holes 7 and 8, 5 and 6. Continue and end at hole 1. Tie the cords together securely.

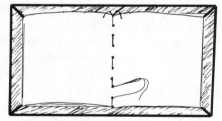

Now the children write on each page and draw their illustrations.

Be sure the title, date, author's name and an attractive illustration are on the cover. Cover illustrations can be cut from construction paper or felt and glued on, or they can be drawn with markers.

Other ideas: A class book is fun to make. Get a large, spiral-bound experience chart. Glue paper on the cover to eliminate the commercial printing and have the children design a title for the book. Let the children write stories and illustrate them.

Reading groups may enjoy keeping a scrapbook of original stories, poems, letters and illustrations to read to other groups. Don't forget to have older children share their literary efforts with younger children and vice versa. It is a good idea to keep a spot in the school library for original books.

Calligraphy (Creative Use of Printed Words)

Color words. Cut a shape from manila paper. Print the word in crayon. Make interesting lines around the letters and use many shades of the color.

Collage

As sounds are introduced, the teacher can cut a large letter from cardboard or heavy paper. Have the children bring pictures that begin with the sound. Glue the sound pictures on the large letter. You will soon have a colorful alphabet. Hang these at the children's eye level around the room, not above the chalkboard. Poster-type collages can be done, using the sound letter and pictures.

Poetry and Illustrations

Children can illustrate poetry with any art medium they like, but haiku poetry is best illustrated with Oriental brush stroke paintings. Older children enjoy learning to brush stroke or print Oriental characters with markers. (Brush stroke painting can be done with a watercolor brush and black watercolor paint.)

Produce a Television Show

A story, news event or a continued series are subject matter. You need a large box, two dowel rods, empty spools and wire or pipe cleaners for the antenna. Use paper that is large enough to be seen and a size that fits the box; 12″ x 28″ or 18″ x 24″ paper can be used or, if the box is large enough, butcher paper works well. Cut a hole in the box an inch smaller than the paper you will use. Paint the box. Leave the back open to change the show. Add spool knobs and antenna. Draw or paint the pictures needed for the presentation.

Tape these together in order with strong masking tape on the back. Tape them to one dowel rod; the last picture is first. Now roll the pictures on this dowel stick. Insert the dowel rod in precut holes in the box. Place the other dowel rod in and pull the first picture over the stick and tape it. Enough extra paper should be left in front of the title picture so the title is centered in the cut-out section.

One or two children operate the show, while others tell the stories to the class. This is a good way to use spoken language.

Creative Action Involves the Whole School Day

Other Creative Language Activities

Make scenery, props and easy costumes for an original play.

Design book jackets. Be sure the ideas are original; never copy a commercial one.

Read a story aloud that has vivid descriptions. Do not show any pictures but have the children draw their interpretations of characters or events in the story.

Read directions in how-to-do-it books and allow the children to make things with as little help from you as possible. The materials they might need should be in the art corner.

Write a story using picture writing or symbols.

Write a story for child-designed puppets. Make them and construct a puppet theater of cardboard.

Art and Social Studies

Social studies curricula go in many directions. Some social studies teachers still use books and follow them closely. Others relate social studies to daily living and its problems or study man in many cultures. One approach involves the study of one topic by the whole school. The teachers select areas and activities that fit their group. When the study is complete there are many projects at various levels to be shared.

Art activities are essential to every social studies unit in any kind of curriculum at every age level. As you plan the material you will teach include murals, drawing, painting, constructing models, collage, weaving, stitchery, printing, ceramics, carving and a study of the culture. Select as many activities as you can do successfully. Vary the kind of projects. Do a mural one time and in another unit make a class book. Model dwellings are meaningful in some units. In others stress the arts and crafts of the groups being studied. Do the projects in class so you know the children have done all the work. How can you do this? Here are some ideas that can be incorporated into any unit.

Drawing and Painting:

Murals—topics and media unlimited
Oriental—calligraphy, drawing and brush painting
People working, playing and living together
African or Egyptian wall paintings
Indian design
Prehistoric cave drawing
Prehistoric worlds and creatures
Animals
Maps

Charts
Posters—travel-type or topic-oriented
People wearing national costumes
Dwellings
Landforms
Environments
Illustrated stories and books
Design inventions

Folk art—Pennsylvania Dutch, Colonial American, Israeli, Portugese, etc.

Cut Paper Activities:

Dress people
Make models of animals, transportation

Construction:

Pariscraft landforms
Dwellings—large enough to walk into or table models
Design new architecture
Dioramas
Models—coal mines, farms, inventions

Write, cast and produce plays—see language arts

Culture of a People:

Arts and crafts—study them and try them

Famous artists and craftsmen

Painting	Printing
Drawing	Music
Weaving	Dance
Stitchery	Language
Ceramics	Literature
Carving	Drama

Architecture—Learn why certain kinds are necessary.
Draw pictures of typical architecture of cities and countries.
Design new cities and buildings.
Topography of land or urban renewal or climate.

Time lines: A time line develops the concept that history is the study of events that happened long ago. With very young children begin with something they remember from a week ago, a month or so, or possibly one year ago. Develop the concept of going back fifty or 100 years and draw pictures of people, inventions or

Creative Action Involves the Whole School Day

events that were important. Glue them along the time line. Make the time line from various colors of construction paper, each color representing a period of time.

Art and Science

Every child who looks into a microscope for a science lesson has expanded his visions of the world. Knowledge grows as new ideas are added and old ideas are improved upon, changed or even discarded. Both artists and scientists experiment to learn new things.

Painting and Drawing

Learning to see—Drawing things observed under a microscope.
Shadow murals—Use with a unit on light. Use a strong light to make shadow drawings of animals or people on mural paper with arms, legs, hands and fingers forming the shadow shapes. Allow these to overlap. Color them.

Using very large mural paper—stand in front of large mural paper as light projects the shadow. Make exaggerated action movements. Have another person trace the figures. Now design and color the shadowed areas.
Draw the seasons or weather, clouds, rain, snow.
Charcoal drawings—Wind, storms, textures.
Watercolor painting—Begin with primary colors and lots of water. Mix these to find new colors. (Color and light unit.)
Crayon resists—Space unit, oceanography unit (sea life).

Drawing (marker or crayon)

>Planets
>Spaceships and space stations
>Explorers
>Inhabitants of outer space
>Space flowers
>Drawings of animals in hibernation
>Fall—open a dried pod and draw the seeds stored for spring that are hidden inside.
>Spring—draw a twig and buds. Two or three weeks later take a twig from the same plant and draw the new growth. Repeat until foliage and blossoms are complete.

Drawing and Design

>Draw a plan for the design of an invention. Build it.
>Construction—Spaceships, space stations, simple machines.
>Casting—Moon's surface—pour plaster into dirt that has been scooped and formed with hands to resemble the ridges, hills, and craters of the moon. When the plaster hardens, brush off the excess dirt.
>Collage—Using colors of cellophane, tissue and construction paper, make a collage on plastic wrap. Put these on the windows to show how light travels through opaque, transparent and translucent materials.
>Make a collage or flower arrangement using dried flowers, weeds and leaves.
>Make a chart of the growth of a seed—Posters, graphs, charts.

Creative Action Involves the Whole School Day

The Five Senses

> Touch—Make a texture collage.
> Hearing—Make a poster showing many kinds of ears, human and animal.
> Sight—Study eyes of insects, animals, humans. Draw technical charts of many
>   kinds.

Rocks

> Collect rocks and use them in terrariums and environment boards.
> Glue rocks of many sizes together to form an animal or imaginary creature.
> Add marker details to natural rock color.

Chlorophyll Drawing

The study of plants is challenging to children at all levels of development. One of the most meaningful ways to teach them about the green substance in plant stems called chlorophyll is to have them draw lines on paper with a juicy, green stem. The warm spring months are ideal times for chlorophyll drawing and this can be done outdoors. The drawings are delicate and smell earthy when they are displayed. When children notice this, point out that chlorophyll is also a deodorant.

Go to a field or have children bring in freshly picked thick-stemmed weeds. Have plenty of 9″ x 12″ newsprint and start drawing with a juicy, cut end of the plant. Keep breaking the stem as you need more color. You will be pleased to see the drawings this inspires. Without being told, children think of plant worlds and insects. These drawings are worthwhile additions to science notebooks.

Art and Mathematics

A close relationship exists here. Math is used in giving directions for many art lessons. Some examples are:

> Take the small paper and fold it in half.
> Use geometric shapes in your design.
> With your brush and water wet a large area on the paper. Leave small
>   sections dry.
> You will need three parts of glue to one part water.
> Use one yard of fabric. Cut it into one-inch strips.
> Measure a cord for macramé so that it is six times as long as you want the
>   finished length.

In all these directions mathematical concepts, terms and ideas are used. Size relationships, ratios and measurements are constantly used in discussing two- or three-dimensional design.

A kindergarten child quickly learns to fold a paper in half, or in two parts, then four parts.

Burlap Counting

Have you a primary group of low-ability math youngsters who have difficulty understanding number concepts? If you combine a few art lessons with a review of math skills, their concepts will be strengthened.

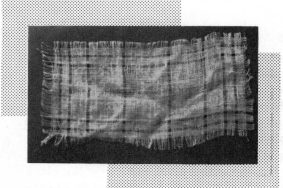

Precut scrap burlap into rectangular shapes, no smaller than 9″, no larger than 15″, about the size of placemats. It is easy for the children to see the individual rows. They should have learned to count by two up to ten previously. Each youngster gets his own piece and sits quietly waiting for instructions. He is going to make a pattern by pulling threads one at a time at first and then two together, but he must follow directions. Each pulled thread is saved so he can check his own work and you can, too.

Everyone counts down six threads and then pulls the next thread from the first side and saves it. The placemat is turned to the next side and the procedure is repeated. Do this on all four sides. Now have the children count six again and pull out two threads. Ask how many ones that is. (Have a straight pin handy in case a thread breaks in the middle and has to be pulled out.) Keep checking to see that directions are being followed.

"Let's make our design prettier. What is an easy way to count bigger numbers? By twos." Practice counting out loud before going on.

Make up patterns such as: Pull out one thread all around and leave four or pull out two and leave eight (count by twos). Some children will be able to work by themselves at this point and can help the others as well. Let them.

Do not have the children work too long. Before they tire, stop. Place a piece of masking tape with each one's name on his piece for identification.

Another day work with different number combinations. Counting by threes, fours or fives can be taught in the same way. A whole set of placemats can be made to be used as gifts. The pulled threads can be saved for sewing, collage or weaving.

Creative Action Involves the Whole School Day

Liquid, Linear and Dry Measures
Are Used in Art Lessons

For instance, after a demonstration, allow the children to measure, mix and pour plaster of Paris and water or allow them to mix Sculptamold using three parts of the dry material to one part water, or ask, "If burlap is one yard wide and two yards long, how many 12″ x 18″ pieces can be cut for the class to use in stitchery?"

Compass, Protractor and Ruler
Designs Are Fun to Make

Plan a color scheme in the shapes that are created. Discuss what colors are made as they blend at intersecting areas. These compass and ruler designs are a way to develop the concept of symmetry. Paper folding and cutting will also produce symmetrical designs.

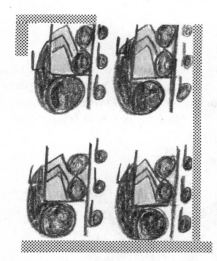

Try a repeated design with numerals such as 6 7 4 8 9. Use a different color for each numeral but repeat the color pattern each time.

Charts and Graphs

These are colorful and more interesting if paint, colored paper, markers or crayon are used. Well-drawn and designed symbols are effective illustrations.

Geometric Shapes

Cylinders, cones, curves, rectangles, squares, circles, ovals, and triangles are all used in 3-D paper constructions.

Fraction Designs

Have the children cut several circles, squares or rectangles from scrap construction paper. These should be drawn with compass and ruler for the sake of mathematical accuracy. Discuss the idea that these are whole parts. Now fold and cut

Creative Action Involves the Whole School Day

them in half. Take another shape and cut it in half and then fold and cut each into four parts. If their shape is large enough they can be divided into even smaller fractional parts. Discuss why one quarter is one part of four parts. Now arrange the many fractional parts into designs and glue them down on a contrasting color of paper.

String Art or Esthiometry

Can straight lines form a curve? Try esthiometry and discover the possibilities by drawing several lines, curves, circles, angles and freeforms and then connecting them. Children should be encouraged to develop their own designs using many kinds of materials and colors. Designs may be done with pencil, ink or marker or they can be stitched with needle and thread.

Begin by drawing two curves or lines. Make dots at small, even intervals along the first one. Number each hole clearly and neatly with a small numerical figure from left to right (or top to bottom). Number the second curve or line the opposite way, from right to left. Connect the numbers. Use a needle to punch the holes. Nails or small tacks may be pounded along the shapes and lines if wood or acoustical tile is used as background. Various string, yarns or wire can be strung to create the overlapping lines. Vary the thickness of these stringing materials for texture and effects of thickness or depth. Textured pieces of driftwood or old wood make interesting backgrounds.

A very simple one-to-one correspondence is a good first lesson.

Next try combining two or three designs in various sizes. Turn the lines or shapes in different directions, overlap them.

Three-dimensional designs may be formed inside painted boxes. These achieve great depth. The more ambitious student can try this after working out a design on paper.

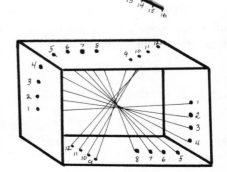

161

Creative Action Involves the Whole School Day

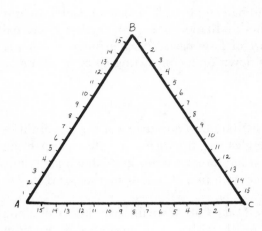

Triangles are done similarly to angles. Start the numbers at each corner. Varying the space between points on the line can alter the effect. Unlimited inventive designs can be worked out.

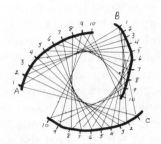

Avoid purchasing prepared kits or following patterns from books. Open or closed curves can be discussed and used in design.

Some books to help you are:

Paper Folding, Donovan A. Johnson; National Council of Teachers of Mathematics

Experiences in Mathematical Discovery–4 Geometry; National Council of Teachers of Mathematics

Designing in String, Robert C. Sharpton; Cuningham Art Product Inc., 1564 McCurdy Dr., Stone Mountain, Ga. 30083

Have a Math Fair

Allow the children to design and execute games using computation skills and numbers. Using many materials such as cardboard, paint, wheels and boards, construct the games and booths. Invite other classes to come to the fair and try them.

Art and Handwriting

What kind of lines do you see? Are there any shapes you know? You might hear these questions during an art lesson, but how about using these same questions in teaching handwriting?

Creative Action Involves the Whole School Day

Did you know that:

S is a curving line and is also a letter?

O is a circle and the letter O?

What is the relationship between c d b a g ?

Printing is really the use of straight lines, curved ones and circular shapes. Help the children see this similarity.

Learning cursive writing is much like line contour drawing. Look at the character you are writing and draw what you see. Eye-hand coordination is an important element in learning handwriting. How important lines are here!

Loops

Connecting circles

Combining forms

Use the ideas in a scribble design on unlined paper.

Tell the children to write in the air to music accompaniment. Play quiet string music to encourage flowing movement. Try a march for the tall letters.

Emphasize that all the tall letters that go above the line should be the same size and those that reach below the line should be equal, too. The letters must be controlled and not go scrawling all over the place. Let the children close their eyes and listen to the music as they write in the air.

Writing is communication, but, like drawing, it takes practice. It is hard to make all the letters slant in the same way. Use the chalkboard. Give several controlled air writers a space on the board and a piece of chalk. Change the group at the chalkboard after a short while so each child has a chance. Have paper for those who are ready for more permanent work. Use wide-lined paper and regular pencils. Now give all the children paper and pencils at their desks. Choose a word that is easy to write, perhaps one with all small letters *car* . Demonstrate on the board Write large and clearly. Change it after a few repetitions to *cat cat cat* . Then *catch* or *catnip* . See if the children are able to follow. Make corrections of a child's work on a separate piece of paper or on the board. Do not obliterate his writing. Make the lesson fun and keep it short enough. Those who wish will practice at lunch time or after school with very little encouragement. Display an example from each student.

Another day teach each person to write his own name. Both first and last names should be used to emphasize individuality and self-worth. Play a game. Have each one write his name and a simple sentence on a piece of paper. Now collect it, put all the samples in a folder, date it and put it away. At the end of the school year have each boy and girl do the same thing without reminding them of their first sample. Pass out the earlier example and let the children evaluate their own progress. Let the students paste and mount both examples on a large design or finger-painting they previously made, which you have saved for this purpose.

Encourage self-evaluation, but do not permit any child to downgrade another's efforts. Give positive comments wherever you can. Some child may now ask for help or be disappointed with his or her handwriting. Here is an example of self-evaluation that can be a step toward self-motivation. Take advantage of it.

Art and Music

As you listen to music you sense movement, rhythm, repetition and mood. As you look at a painting you sense the same things. Music and art are closely related and should reinforce one another.

Drawings will become free and rhythmic if the children listen to music as they draw. It is interesting to paint the rhythm of the music with brush strokes. There will be short choppy lines, smooth ones and long soaring ones if the children really listen and interpret the music.

Have your music teacher suggest material that expresses obvious moods. Collect happy sounds, sad ones, funny music or other effects. These will help create moods for painting. Exciting music stimulates us as we create in a different way than soothing music does.

Draw pictures to show how music makes you feel. Select music that is descriptive such as:

"The Sugar Plum Fairy" from *The Nutcracker Suite*
"The Mountain King" from *The Peer Gynt Suite*
Pictures at an Exhibition—Moussorgsky
Carnival of the Animals—Saint-Saens

Creative Action Involves the Whole School Day

Draw or paint the way these people or animals would look. Listen to *Peter and the Wolf*. Draw a scene for each part of the story.

Before a trip to a concert, obtain a program and listen to recordings that will be played. Ask the orchestra or band teacher to bring in as many instruments as possible. Allow the children to examine them. There are large card sets of orchestra instruments that are useful, too. Discuss the curves, shapes, sizes, textures and colors of the instruments.

Creative Action Involves the Whole School Day

Have the children make large line drawings of instruments drawing as much detail as they can. Make a book of these drawings. After the trip allow the children to paint or draw a picture that shows their impression of their favorite music. Write stories about the trip. Put these in the book and keep it as a memorable record of their concert trip.

Make original instruments from found materials. See if they can make sounds.

How does a picture sound? This is a reverse of drawing a picture of music. In music and dance or body movement, interpret a picture or frieze that tells a story (Diego Rivera murals, Aztec, Egyptian, city murals).

Draw or paint pictures that interpret song titles or folk songs.

Art and Physical Education

Ask the physical education teacher if your class can sketch gym groups in outdoor activities, track events, playing on jungle gyms, baseball, football, races. This is a good place to watch figures in action following the lesson in chapter 3. Draw one or many action figures.

Cut out shapes from manila paper. Discuss body movement. Fit a figure into the shape filling the space as if the body were closed in.

Have a child hold a dance position in front of a strong light while someone traces the shadow on large paper. Show many dance forms—square dance, ballet poses, interpretive movement.

Watch a class tumbling and doing gymnastics. Relate these to a circus acrobatic team. Paint a circus as a whole having the acrobats performing with others.

Pyramids—create new patterns for these gymnastic structures. Remember shape and balance as you design.

Draw diagrams of sports—football, hockey, baseball, etc.

Make collages of sports and sports figures.

11 Dust the Cobwebs Off the Bulletin Board

We all spend much time, care and thought in choosing paintings, drawings or wall hangings for our homes. We want them to reflect our taste, our personality and the atmosphere of our surroundings. Bulletin boards and display areas are just as important to the beauty and personality of our school environment, so dust the cobwebs off the bulletin boards and out of your mind. Keep displays innovative and attractive. Change them often and have them reflect areas of study and the interests of the class. Fresh ideas and new materials take the "bored" out of bulletin boards!

Easy Changes in Classroom Display

There will be at least three kinds of bulletin boards in your room.

Permanent Displays

Usually one area in a room has a helper chart or lists, committees, graphs or records of some sort. Primary rooms have calendar work as part of mathematics.

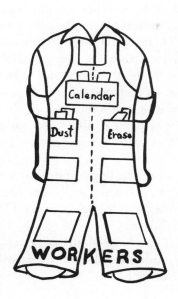

Objects mounted on these display areas could be made of cardboard or clear Con-Tact paper to enable you to wipe off crayon marks to change names. Using dry mount and lamination techniques lengthens the life of the display. Use fadeless paper. Think of clever ways to caption and illustrate such bulletin boards. Have the class help.

Teaching Displays

An area of the room with a table and display area can be used to introduce lessons, provide thought-provoking ideas and display collections. Put books, magazines and objects on the table and mount the materials, pictures or directions above them as the unit develops.

Dust the Cobwebs Off the Bulletin Board

Changing Displays

If you have an art corner, allow the children to be creative and provide storage space for their work. You will have more bulletin board material than you will use. Change these displays as often as possible. Vary the kinds of background and mounting. Use short, clear, catchy titles. Print or write the captions on shapes or on strips of paper. Do not waste your time cutting individual, involved letters.

Avoid holiday themes or monthly topics that are bound by the passing of time to change whether you are ready or not. Valentine themes are not applicable or even appropriate by February 15, so why display hearts, flowers and pink, red and white materials for one day? An exchange of handmade Valentine cards and a small party at the end of the afternoon is much more personal. Use your display areas innovatively. There is nothing as unattractive as an outdated bulletin board.

Do not be limited by the size of a bulletin board. Allow the material to extend beyond the edges at the top, bottom and sides. Do not put work that you want children to see too far above or below their eye level. Use large objects that can be seen from a distance wherever possible. If you are studying the circus, for example, make clowns seven feet tall, or three feet wide. Display a huge elephant decked out for a circus parade. Big, bold, colorful objects attract attention!

Use yarn or linear shapes to move the eye from place to place on your bulletin board.

Avoid scalloped borders and edging around bulletin boards. These compete for attention with the objects on display and confine you to the space within its boundaries. Let the ideas expand by also using the wall area outside the border of the bulletin board.

If you have plenty of floor space, have the children make very large constructions or build model homes, spaceships or huge imaginary animals, which help create an environment.

New Ways to Display Children's Work

Let's consider some ways to display children's work that go beyond attaching a flat piece to a bulletin board.

Dust the Cobwebs Off the Bulletin Board

Small shelves can be made from corrugated boxes. Cut across the top and corners. Then cut at an angle to form supporting sides. Paint them in neutral, attractive colors. Keep plenty of sizes available. These can be tacked on bulletin boards to hold three-dimensional objects and lightweight constructions. The shelf can be turned upside down, too.

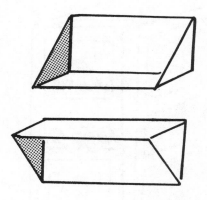

Construct 12″ x 18″ easels of corrugated cardboard and place them on shelves to display weaving, stitchery or other art work.

Paint some large, strong, grocery boxes and use these as a kiosk for free-standing displays. Put flat work on all four sides and a three-dimensional piece on top. Pictures can be pinned to the cardboard. Use several kiosks of varied height in interesting groupings in a section of the room.

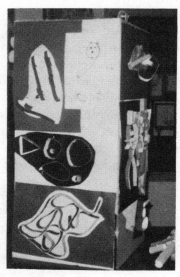

In narrow areas between windows, aluminum strips with cork inserts can be mounted on the walls. Panels of burlap stapled to these form colorful display areas. Pictures and stitchery projects can be pinned to the burlap hangings. Butcher paper strips can be used instead of burlap.

Cover or paint a tall, thin box, weighted inside with a brick. Place it at an end of a shelf to display three-dimensional work on top and paintings and designs on the sides. Tape or staple a strip of burlap to the top of the shelf and hang it behind the box to display more art work.

Save the small boxes that have been covered or painted to add elevation to other displays the children use in social studies, science and math.

The aluminum and cork strips (in longer lengths) can be spaced to accommodate murals and large pictures. Strips are cheaper than a bulletin board and less obtrusive when they are not in use.

Many teachers secure a small tree in a container of plaster of Paris. These are attractive display areas for mobile-type three-dimensional paper constructions. As they turn and float they add a colorful, graceful spot in the room.

Be observant as you walk through tastefully decorated shopping centers and department stores. Quite often you will see a new way to display objects that can be adapted to the classroom.

Remember to keep your room environment fresh, inspiring and innovative.

Dust the Cobwebs Off the Bulletin Board

Use Your Entire Room

There's no display space in your room, you say? With some brainstorming you and the class will find areas not usually used as hanging space that can turn your room into an exciting place to work and learn.

Don't limit yourself to the conventional bulletin board. Do you have metal cabinets, lockers, bookcases or metal desks? Get several dozen plain, undecorated magnets and magnetic strips. Use them to attach paper work to any metal surface, but remember to use four to anchor each piece of work. Use the sides and back of any metal surface you find. Make interesting groupings rather than ordinary rows of work.

If you have wooden furniture, glue cork sections or strips over some of the surfaces and use straight pins to hold the art work. There still are other possibilities. Use the doors, shelves and the space over the lockers. Try to keep any material that is to be read at the seated child's eye level. Save higher spaces for design work.

Have you considered the beams, ceilings and light fixtures? Hang mobiles so that they aren't too low or in a drafty area.

Use the wall space between windows. Two concrete or wood nails hammered in (with permission) at a forty-five degree angle make a support for a removable burlap bulletin board. The easiest way to make one is to stitch a seam at the top of a piece of burlap that is slightly wider than a standard dowel stick from the hardware store. Straight pins are used to attach the art work.

To vary your room decor, change the display or the color of the burlap. Take it down and hang some charts, a wall hanging or a banner on the nails.

What about the windows? Use Metylan to attach the pictures.

For special exhibits use table tops and painted grocery boxes.

Don't overdo it. We are trying to teach the children esthetic values and good taste. It is better to change small displays frequently than to have every wall and spot covered with things for long periods of time. When this happens, you don't see anything but clutter. Save some empty space in a quiet area.

Look for Different Display Areas

Why confine all the good displays to your classroom? Find different display areas.

Who is in charge of arranging exhibits in the school showcases, library, cabinets, lunchroom, teachers' lounge, office, front hall and general hallways? Ask if you can share a particularly good art display. Pretrain display teams of two or three children to put up and remove exhibits. If you teach primary grades, get older children to help. If you enjoy creating displays, help them. If not, get an enthusiastic group that works well together. Show them the materials and let them innovate. Set a time limit and keep it. One hour is usually sufficient if all the materials needed have been grouped in advance.

Stained glass window effects are very dramatic. See chapter 4 for ways to create some.

If there is a courtyard, perhaps an outdoor art fair can be arranged. Many local libraries, banks, clinics, hospitals, and some shopping centers look for outside exhibits. Find out. Adults usually enjoy the free, cheerful art work of children. P.T.A. groups may offer some help with phone calls, leg work, setting up exhibits, and making arrangements.

Backgrounds—Temporary and Permanent

In the junior high it seems as if very little attention is paid to room appearance and decor. Everything is impersonal. Few rooms other than the art room, the library, the office, the home economics areas and perhaps the music room are decorated in any way. We seem to be teaching the children that esthetics don't matter.

A permanent wall mural can be designed to incorporate symbols in any subject field to enhance the dullest wall. Why not ask the art department to have a group of youngsters design and execute an original mural for your junior high room?

In the elementary school room it is better to have temporary backgrounds that are changed frequently. Burlap or butcher paper that has been first pinned and then stapled to a bulletin board makes an excellent background. A neutral color is easiest to use as a semipermanent display setting. Thin, colored corrugated cardboard is another material some teachers like. Pins, rather than tacks or staples, are needed to hold the displays on corrugated surfaces.

The schoolroom walls are possible backgrounds. Choose an inside or warm wall if possible. Use masking tape, rolled into circles with the sticky side out, not cellophane tape, on the back of picture corners and press them to the wall. Keep the pictures fairly close together in simple groupings to minimize the wall texture or design, which can be distracting.

Con-Tact paper cut into simple curved forms and pasted on doors or untextured surfaces provides interesting background variations from the usual construction paper backdrop. Try very plain Wall-Tex fabric or shelf paper pasted on cardboard and then hung on the walls as a background, too. Some of the simpler finger paintings can be backgrounds for poetry or other language arts work.

If it is included in your budget, fadeless paper is an excellent semipermanent backing for displaying any school work.

Permanent backgrounds can be made in many ways. Planned murals that are painted directly on the walls or on panels to be hung in the halls will make your school a place the boys and girls can be proud of. Ceramic tiles or clay wall hangings are attractive, too. Use massive wood collages hung in unattractive areas to enhance those areas. Large pieces of wood sculpture can be constructed for a niche in the hallway or an entrance corner.

Dust the Cobwebs Off the Bulletin Board

Groups of upper-grade students like to work on permanent wall displays so that when they have graduated, they can always come back to the school and find that they still belong.

Use your imagination to combine ideas. There is never an end to that source of supply. Build on ideas.

12 Materials Matter: What's Junk to Some Is Treasure to Others

Mill ends . . . scrap tile . . . unwanted slides . . . bamboo . . . carpeting . . . poles . . . odd pieces of wallboard and paneling. . . . Who wants this junk? You do! What's junk to some is treasure to others.

Parents, neighbors and other teachers and your art supervisor will help you stock your closets with scrap materials *if* they know what you are looking for. At the beginning of each school year prepare a note to go home with each student asking for:

scrap fabric	plastic bags
buttons	empty spools
baby food jars	egg cartons
textured paper	Styrofoam meat trays
tile	empty containers
small pieces of wood, leather, yarn	cardboard
plastic odds and ends	Styrofoam packing pieces
rug scraps	coffee and orange juice cans

Often a parent works for a company that will be glad to donate scrap items that will become the inspiration for many art sessions. Don't underestimate a child's imagination or your own. Keep a box of scrap materials and plan lessons for its specific use. Your librarian may also know of free sources of material. Ask.

Have a place to put your treasures where the children can see them and use them. Trade excess items with another class. Here is an unlimited source of free supplies.

Any teacher who teaches art finds that one of her best friends in the school building is the custodian. Without his help and cooperation many exciting art ideas and plans would have to be scrapped. Who else saves huge pieces of cardboard and helps cut them to size, or finds cartons, jars, buckets and dropcloths when no one else can? Is there a better way of getting a small amount of solvent in an emergency? Is there anyone else in the school building who is more capable of showing a group of interested youngsters how to use basic tools? To keep him as a friend make sure art materials are kept off the floor, table tops and out of the sink drain. Have the class plan a workable cleanup schedule and follow it.

Traditional Materials

What art materials are basic? Almost any school supply list will include crayons, glue and scissors. These traditional items must be of good quality because they are in daily use. In ordering, specify brand names, sizes and quantities you find work best for the age group you teach. Beyond these basics a teacher should have as many of the following art supplies as possible for drawing and painting.

Drawing—Save as many used drawing tools as you can.
    Crayons—unwrapped, scrap crayons
    Pencils—soft lead (primary pencils are good)
    Charcoal—in various sizes and widths
    Chalk—colored and white
    Markers—permanent ink
Paper cutter
Scissors—pointed, sharp enough to cut paper and fabric
Painting—tempera, poster paint, or powdered tempera
    Fingerpaint
    Watercolor sets
    Acrylics in jars
    Brushes—all of good quality with seamless, nonrusting ferrules.
        small, soft hair brushes
        large, soft hair brushes
        stiff easel brushes
    Cans for water and paint
Polymer
Glue and Metylan art paste
Paper—in most schools budgets are tight, so 12″ x 18″ paper is a size that can be used frequently or cut into smaller pieces. You will need a supply of these papers:

newsprint	butcher roll-type paper
manila	white drawing paper
assorted colors of	finger-paint paper
construction paper	

A good art program is developed by a creative tacher who uses what he or she has to help the children learn skills and techniques. A closet full of expensive art materials does not assure a fine program. Keep developing your teaching abilities and have an open mind toward new or substitute materials, ideas and techniques.

Scrap Materials—What's Useful?

Almost anything is useful in some way in art if you develop a creative attitude. Ask yourself, "What new use can I give this material?"

Dryer lint is clean, free and makes great stuffing for puppets, animals and birds.

Materials Matter

The little circles and rectangles from hole punchers and IBM cards are good additions to collage. They come in various colors, too.

Notions—ribbon binding, rickrack, braid, trims, buttons, sequins, frames from trims (for looms) are handy extras.

Scrap pieces of rugs and fabrics can be used in collage, stitchery, and cut into strips for weaving. What better mane could a papier-mâché or Pariscraft lion have than a piece of shag rug?

Carpet samples are useful for collage and add texture to almost anything.

Yarn scraps and odds and ends include many more colors and textures than you can buy.

Wood scraps—the industrial arts teacher in the junior or senior high school can give you many shapes and kinds.

Lumber—in addition to scrap wood, don't forget to ask for sawdust and wood curls.

Frame pieces—picture frame scraps have interesting colors and textures. Scraps of matboard and cardboard have possibilities.

Cardboard—have the custodian save large boxes. Be on the lookout for appliance cartons for large projects.

Covers or backs from notebook paper, legal pads, spiral notebooks, notepads and shirt board are useful for printmaking and mounting pictures.

Boxes from department stores are valuable for displaying and storage.

Plastic lids from spray cans, toothpaste tops, Airwick room freshener tops and bottle caps can be used creatively in a three-dimensional collage on scrap wood. This is a good lesson to stress size relationships, form and texture. These can be left as they are or spray painted.

Styrofoam cases that are formed to fit the object they protect come from appliances, radios and recording equipment. These can be painted with acrylics and used as wall decorations or broken or cut to use in constructions.

Styrofoam pellets are packing pieces that come in unbelievable sizes, shapes and colors. They are fun to make into jewelry, abstract constructions or used in collages.

Styrofoam meat trays can be used for printmaking or stitchery. Egg cartons of the same material are useful as paint containers, chalk or crayon holders or can be used in construction.

Leather or bits of fur or suede make handsome additions to collage work or stitchery. Strips can be used for macramé, weaving and wall hangings as well as jewelry.

Wrapping paper can be incorporated in pictures or designs emphasizing texture, shine or color.

Paper bags can be made into puppets and Indian costumes.

Printing companies have ends of heavy, fine-quality paper in good colors. Rolls of paper are best for murals.

Wallpaper books have possibilities as parts of collage for color or texture. The pages of Wall-Tex and other sturdy papers are wonderful for desk covers and to work on with clay.

Old TV tray legs are ideal rug or burlap frames. Sew the edges around the open top frame. It can be opened and made taut or closed for flat storage.

Materials Matter

Needle substitutes—for very large weaving spaces cut a corrugated cardboard needle or shuttle.

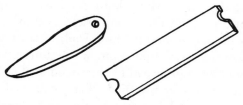

Round toothpicks can be used to push yarn into Styrofoam for designs. Masking tape tightly wrapped around the end of a piece of yarn is useful for some kinds of stitchery. Colorless nail polish seals yarn ends, too. Punch holes in the paper for simple stitchery. Mesh potato bags are good for weaving.

New Materials

Each year new materials appear in the art catalogs. Some are advances made possible by scientific discoveries while others are merely gimmicks or ways to add frills to your budget. Few companies send free samples any more and reading an advertising pamphlet is no substitute for actually trying the new material. If you are able to attend a workshop or an in-service art program, participate in an actual demonstration or visit an art convention or materials show, you will find new products and ideas suitable for your grade level and your own art adventures. Your art coordinator should be able to suggest brand names, too.

Some new materials you will be enthusiastic about are:

Sculptamold	Polymer
Metylan art paste	Tempera cakes
Pariscraft	Fadeless paper
Acrylic paint	Dubl-Hue paper
Watercolor sticks	School ecology paper
Paint sticks	

Sculptamold

What material is pliable to work with but dries hard, can be used for a low-relief effect, can be painted or used with markers, will adhere to wood, cardboard, glass, foil, dries white and doesn't have an odor? In a scientific experiment testing many samples of synthetic products, the boys and girls chose a cellulose material called Sculptamold as the one they liked best.

Sculptamold comes as a powder that is mixed with water several minutes before it is needed. Use your hands or a spatula if you prefer. It should feel like soft dough while it is being handled. Do some experimental mixing with a small group of children using about two cups of Sculptamold in a plastic or metal bowl and a half cup of cold water. Add more water if necessary but don't add more Sculptamold. It acts as a catalyst and hardens too quickly. Have baby food jars, buttons, small pieces of Styrofoam trays, clean but used tin foil, small sticks and other scrap pieces for the children to experiment with and imbed in their Sculptamold or formed shapes. Use oilcloth to cover the desk, give each child some of the doughlike material and let the fun begin. Sculptamold will become warm to the touch as it starts to harden. Do not make more than the group will use at one time. If an additional amount is needed in a hurry, use the uncleaned mixing bowl to mix the next batch. Let the remaining particles in the bowl act as a catalyst. The new mixture will set up, like plaster of Paris, in about five minutes. If there is no rush and the children wish to experiment, be sure to wipe out the bowl with a paper towel or cloth before mixing more.

Show the group that as the Sculptamold gets drier it can be molded around an object such as baby food jars, can have objects imbedded in it for texture and designs can be drawn into the surface with sticks or pencils after it has been smoothed with dampened fingers. Let the pieces dry on waxed paper on the windowsill or on an open shelf. If a piece should break or crack, mix up a small amount of Sculptamold and repair it. It can also be glued with white glue.

All the pieces will shrink slightly so imbed any armature (wire or other support) well and make sure pieces of Styrofoam are pushed in so they will not fall out later.

Any art project containing quantities of water should be made on a dry day.

Puppet heads, jewelry, beads, topographical maps, bas reliefs and sculpture are some of the many uses of this versatile material. Stress good workmanship.

An informative booklet about Sculptamold can be purchased and leaflets with other suggestions are available at your art supply store.

For cleanup, rub the hands free of loose pieces over a wastebasket. Use up any extra pieces of Sculptamold so there are no leftovers, or discard particles as you would tin cans as Sculptamold does not burn. Be careful not to let any pieces go down the drain. Use a metal scraper or wooden stick to remove anything that may have dropped on the floor.

In a day or two, when the pieces are thoroughly dry, paint or color them with any medium. Polymer can be used as a final coat.

Metylan Art Paste

Here is a product you may prefer in many cases to other adhesives such as wheat paste, white glue and school paste. It is very easy to use, is versatile and requires less storage space. Mice don't seem to like it as they do wheat paste. Metylan is smooth, clean, has no odor, leaves no film on the desk or paper, and is water soluble. Kindergarten teachers are delighted that it doesn't spill or crumble.

It comes in powder form and you can mix small or large quantities depending

Materials Matter

upon your needs. Metylan stores well in tightly closed wide-necked plastic containers such as margarine-type tubs. Never use metal containers or the product will become too watery. A good recipe to follow is:

> 1½ tsp. Metylan
> ½ cup of water

You can easily double or triple the amount. Stir with a stick or spatula to dissolve. Let it sit ten minutes before using. Children like to use their fingers to apply it.

Try Metylan for papier-mâché, collage, découpage, tissue-paper designs, mounting pictures to paper and for mounting paper to glass windows.

Pariscraft

To create textures, relief maps, three-dimensional work or to cover or stiffen something, use the plaster-impregnated gauze tape that has been used by doctors for plaster casts for years. It is called Pariscraft and comes by the carton in rolls of varied widths.

Precut the Pariscraft with a paper cutter to sizes and lengths suitable for each project. Be sure to use newspaper both under the paper cutter and on the floor to catch the plaster dust. Use gallon milk cartons cut down to about three or four inches to hold the small amount of water needed to moisten and soften the gauze. Spread newspapers as desk coverings to facilitate cleanup.

For primary children you may prefer to use large, flat, plastic pans instead of a milk carton. Put the pan on a table between four children. Hold one edge of a piece of Pariscraft with both hands. Dip the piece into the water and hold it above the pan until the dripping stops. Lay the piece of Pariscraft on the object.

Have the object to be covered ready. One layer of Pariscraft usually is enough. Small strips are easiest to handle but when covering huge objects larger pieces take less time. Dip one piece at a time into the cold water. Remove it immediately and do not let it soak. Squeeze the water back into the milk container. Carefully open the entire piece, put it on the object to be covered and use fingers to smooth it out. Use as little water as possible. Avoid putting on pieces that are dripping wet. All the ends of one strip should meld into the next and no seam should be visible. This is important. Remember that plaster must not go into the sink and that it does not burn. At the end of a lesson any small amount of residue in the containers can be discarded or used immediately in a craft project.

Avoid using Pariscraft during wet weather. Finished Pariscraft pieces should be stored to dry on a shelf, desk or window ledge, not in a closed area. Pariscraft objects can be painted while wet as soon as the material begins to harden. Tempera, watercolor, stain, markers and acrylic paint all work well on this material. Objects like string, beads and rickrack can be imbedded in the gauze for special effects or glued on later.

If the Pariscraft is to be put on cardboard, as for a topographical relief map, first protect the cardboard with a coat of glue or acrylic paint so that it doesn't get waterlogged. Aluminum foil forms are good sculptural bases. Possibilities for using Pariscraft are unlimited. It is one of the most valuable new art products we have.

Acrylic Paint

What is water-soluble when wet and permanent when dry? Acrylic paint.

Not too long ago your group finished painting a beautiful backdrop for your play or a mural for that important unit. The children used tempera paint because once they used chalk and it got all over the room, in the air and rubbed off on everyone's clothing before you had time to take it outdoors to spray it. The tempera was dry and you were going to hang it up when Susie, who is so uncoordinated, tripped on the jar of water and spilled it all over. All the colors ran. That was that.

If you had used acrylics, nothing would have been spoiled. Acrylic paint in jars is best for elementary grades. Sets in tubes can be purchased for adults and older children.

Use acrylic paint as you would use tempera but make sure everyone wears a long smock to cover his or her clothing. Remember, when it is dry, it is permanent. That goes for brushes, too. Wash brushes in water immediately after use. Keep a coffee can half full of water ready to put the brushes in. Even if there is only a five-minute break in the lesson (like a fire drill) the brushes must be submerged.

Use a sponge or rag to clean up drips while they are wet. In an emergency isopropyl alcohol will help remove acrylic paint.

Acrylics will cover many surfaces where tempera will chip or slide off. Use them for posters, paintings, murals, scenery, rock painting, Styrofoam painting, or on wood, metal, glass or plastic. Try acrylics on papier-mâché, Pariscraft and Sculptamold or in combination with collage.

Experiment with acrylics as a background for printmaking, cutting and pasting or markers.

Watercolor Sticks

Interesting effects can be gotten using watercolor sticks and traditional watercolor techniques. Experiment to find new ways to paint.

Paint Sticks

These are oil-based, chunky, crayonlike sticks. Heavy, textural effects can be gotten with these and they are easy to blend. Paint sticks are soft when applied but dry to a hard finish.

Materials Matter

Polymer

Polymer is a liquid product that is water-soluble when wet and permanent when dry. Use polymer:

As final coating where varnish or shellac would ordinarily be used as a sealer.

To adhere tissue paper to itself, to jars or to anything else.

On papier-mâché—Try covering the dry, finished art project with a coat and then use markers on top of the dry polymer. No finishing coat of polymer is necessary.

Add a few drops to tempera to make the paint more permanent where acrylics are not available.

Polymer now comes in plastic containers. It looks and pours like white glue but dries clear. Both matte (dull) and glossy finishes are available. Be sure to carefully wipe the rim and cover of the container before closing it. Some brands of polymer can be diluted while others must be used full strength. Until you've used it, you won't know how many uses polymer has.

Be sure to wash brushes with soap and water while they are still wet. An easy way to ruin a brush is to let polymer, white glue or acrylic paint dry on the bristles. An easy way to clean the brush is to do it while wet.

Tempera Cakes

Tempera paint is now made in a semisolid form. Several companies sell sets of a dozen or more colors in plastic tray containers. Drop a bit of water on top of each cake and paint away. The colors are clear, can be blended and require no advance jar opening or pouring of paint into containers. Cleanup is simple; just blot off each color with a paper towel before putting the set away. Replacement colors are available. A transparent watercolor or opaque tempera effect or a combination of techniques can easily be created depending on the amount of water and paint used.

In addition to paint and color quality, look for newer and better pliable plastic containers. These may cost slightly more but will be more durable. The containers stack easily and take less shelf space than jars of tempera.

Fadeless Paper

Construction paper fades when it is exposed to light. A beautiful bulletin board or attractive display can look unattractive after a week unless you use fadeless paper. There is a difference in price but you may find it better to economize in other ways. Use this special art material carefully. Save the colored scraps for other lessons and never permit the children to waste or use it as scrap writing paper. One package or several dozen pieces can go a long way. Marker lines are dark and clear against the brightly colored, smooth surface. Posters and collages are even more effective using fadeless paper.

Dubl-Hue Paper

Dubl-Hue is two-toned construction-weight paper. Each side has a color shade or complementary color. It is a versatile material to use for three-dimensional paper designs, mobiles and window displays. Try this interesting paper for special effects. Use it only when both sides will be visible. It is more expensive than construction paper; do not use it as a substitute.

School Ecology Paper

Using recycled construction paper is a good way to economize. The quality is comparable to a medium-quality school paper.

Ask for color swatches and order only the attractive colors in ecology-type paper. If a particular color is dull or unpleasant, substitute the regular construction paper. In that way you can save some money and still have the colors you need.

Free or Inexpensive Materials— Where and How to Obtain Them

There are still free materials that can be yours if you know how to obtain them. Many art magazines list advertisers who will send booklets and sometimes even samples that are free or nominal in cost. Look through the lists of free product information and send for what appeals to you. The magazine *Learning–The Magazine for Creative Teaching* (Education Today Company, Inc., 80 Park Street, Montclair, New Jersey 07042) has an excellent list of free or low-cost resources.

Other fine publications can be obtained from the following companies:

Amaco
(Series HH-6)
(booklets)
Fingerpaint—ask for a list of their publications.

Indianapolis, Indiana 46222

The American Crayon Co.
Everyday Art (beautiful booklets)

Sandusky, Ohio 44870

Binney & Smith, Inc.
A portfolio of suggestions for use in your art education program

380 Madison Avenue
New York, New York 10017

Materials Matter

Coats & Clark, Inc.
The ABC of Crochet—basic stitches,
charts, crochet projects, booklet

1701 Pollitt Drive
Fair Lawn, New Jersey 07410

Fibrec
How to Tie & Dye (booklet)

2795 16th Street
San Francisco, California 94103

Grumbacher, Inc.
Palette Talk (small magazine)

486 West 34th Street
New York, New York 10001

Hunt Manufacturing Co.
Acrylic & Polymer
Painting (booklet)

1305 Locust Street
Philadelphia, Pennsylvania 19102

Lily Mills
Basic Stitches for Creative
Stitchery (large wall chart)

Educational Division
Shelby, North Carolina

National Gallery of Art
A Catalog of Reproductions &
Publications

Washington, D.C. 20565

Permanent Pigments, Inc.
Liquitex Techniques (pamphlets)

2700 Highland Avenue
Cincinnati, Ohio 45212

Rit Consumer Service Dept.
Dye-Craft ideas (booklet)

Best Foods Division
CPC International Inc.
1427 West Morris Street
Indianapolis, Indiana 46206
or
Box 307
Dept. GL-S
Coventry, Connecticut 06238

Sta-Flo Liquid Starch
Fun with Sta-Flo Liquid Starch
(booklet)

Decatur, Illinois

Tandy Leather Co.
A new look at leather—
An Approach for the Art Teacher
(booklet)

P.O. Box 791
Fort Worth, Texas 76101
(or local Tandy Craft Stores)

Tri-Wall Containers, Inc.
Cardboard Carpentry (booklet)

1 Dupont Street
Plainview, New York 11802

Several companies offer good source materials such as charts, booklets and
how-to ideas. When you write, use school stationery and also ask about other availa-

ble free material. Be selective about the information you receive. Use only the creative ideas and discard the trite. Look for ideas using fresh, stimulating ways to use art skills combining creative thought and new materials.

Your public library is one of the most neglected sources of free materials. Librarians are trained to assist you. The head librarian welcomes your suggestions about books you would like to see in the library. Through outright purchase or interlibrary exchanges you can get what you need.

It is worthwhile to buy copies of one or more of the following:

Beautiful Junk (free)	Diane Warner & Jeanne Quilk Project HeadStart Office of Child Development Dept. of Health, Education & Welfare P.O. Box 1182 Washington, D.C. 20013
Catalog of Free Teaching Materials	P.O. Box 1075 Ventura, California
Free & Inexpensive Educational Materials (cost $2.00)	Thomas Pepe Dover Publishing Co.
Free & Inexpensive Learning Materials (cost $3.00)	George Peabody College Division of Survey & Field Services Nashville, Tennessee 37203
Free & Inexpensive Things for Teens (cost $.75)	Mark Weiss Scholastic Book Services
Trash to Treasure (cost $1.00)	Sue McCord Project Change State University of New York Cortland, New York 13045

Films

Did you know that there are several outstanding films for classroom use that you can borrow without cost? Some libraries lend films. Check with the local one and find out if there is a program that enables you to borrow films from other libraries.

Your own school may have a film, filmstrip and slide library or your district may have a separte collection. Large corporations often make special films available to schools. The local Bell Telephone business office lends films. Your state museum library has hundreds of films to borrow for one specified day. Associated Sterling Films, 512 Burlington Avenue, LaGrange, Illinois 60525, has an excellent film, *Art Is* (reserve four months in advance).

Materials Matter

Filmstrips

Filmstrips are inexpensive motivational or supplementary materials. There are many escellent titles on the market and a number of poor ones. Some come with records, books, cassettes, pamphlets or other explanatory materials. The difference in price between a really good filmstrip and a poor one may be nonexistent or nominal. Expect to pay ten to twenty dollars for each filmstrip including its supplementary materials. Similar subject matter from different companies should be compared before you purchase. Ask for preview privileges. Beware of special offers of very inexpensive filmstrips from teacher's magazines. These are hardly worth what you pay for them.

It is not always necessary to buy an entire series or even both parts of a two-part set. You may find that one is enough or that the second or third filmstrip is repetitious or not as well done as the first. Choose just what you need. Economize in this way, not through buying an inferior product.

Some excellent filmstrips are:

Filmstrip	Book	Record	Manual	Company	Grade*
Construction	xx		xx	Western Publishing Co.	M, U
Painting	*xx*		*xx*	" " "	"
Paper Art	xx		xx	" " "	"
Papier-Mâché	xx		xx	" " "	"
Print Art	xx		xx	" " "	"
Stitchery	xx		xx	" " "	"
Africa—					
Architecture		xx		Warren Schloat	"
Culture		xx		" "	"
Jewelry		xx		" "	"
Masks		xx		" "	"
Sculpture		xx		" "	"
Textiles		xx		" "	"
Children of UNICEF		xx		" "	P,M,U
Africa		xx		" "	"
Latin America		xx		" "	"
Famous Artists		xx		" "	M, U
Individual Persons					
The Middle Ages,					
Part 1		xx		" "	U
Emphasis Art			xx	International Film Bureau	M, U
Creative Approaches Processes in Leather				Tandy Leather Co.	M, U

*Grade—M (middle, 3 and 4), U (5 and up), P (K, 1 and 2)

Informative catalogs can be obtained from:

A.C.I. Films, Inc.
35 W. 45 Street
New York, N.Y. 10036

BFA Educational Media
2211 Michigan Avenue
Santa Monica, California 90104

Coronet (Perspective Films)
369 W. Erie Street
Chicago, Illinois 60610

Educational Dimensions Corporation
Box 488
Great Neck, New York 11022

Encyclopedia Brittanica
425 N. Michigan
Chicago, Illinois 60611

International Film Bureau
332 South Michigan Avenue
Chicago, Illinois 60604

Warren Schloat
115 Tompkins Avenue
Pleasantville, New York 10570

Western Publishing Co., Inc.
Educational Div. School and Library Dept.
150 Parish Drive
Wayne, New Jersey 07470

13 Use What You Have and Get What You Can

Audio-Visual Equipment

Most schools have audio-visual equipment, but unfortunately the machines often go unused. Teachers are afraid to try these aids, have not been instructed in their use, or don't have time to learn. Find out exactly what equipment you have available and use audio-visual aids as a supplement to your teaching. When you feel comfortable using the machines, teach the children to operate them, too. You will find the equipment valuable when you introduce lessons, develop skills and review material. Movies, filmstrips, slides and transparencies capture the attention of your class if they are used as an integral part of units and subject matter. Never use an audio-visual aid as a baby sitter or a time filler.

The Overhead Projector

This machine is versatile and easy to use. Once you try it you will discover its unlimited potential. An overhead projector uses incline mirrors and a strong light to project material from a glass, tablelike surface called a stage.

The overhead projector is portable.
It can be used in a lighted room.
The teacher faces her group at all times.
The projector is easily turned on and off to focus attention to the material and then back to the speaker.
Teacher and children can create their own material for lessons.
Supplies used to make transparencies are simple and inexpensive.

What materials are needed?

The overhead projector
A screen (a piece of white paper or large cardboard will do if a commercial screen is not available.)
Transparency sheets or a roll of transparency film attached to the projector.
A nylon-tipped permanent marker or grease pencil. Pretest these to be sure they make a dark, even line.

Using the overhead projector:

Have your materals ready in the order you wish to use them.

Check the transparencies on the projector to be sure the machine is set up
properly and in focus before the lesson, then you never have to look at
the projected material, only at the class.

Have a pencil to use as a pointer.

With a nylon-tipped black marker or a grease pencil handy you or the children may mark on the transparency as the lesson progresses.

If you use commercially prepared transparencies, draw or write on a separate
sheet of film so that the original can be reused.

Be sure each member of the class can see and no one has to look around the
projector.

Put your material on the stage of the projector before you turn on the light.
Turn off the light as you change transparencies, so the bright, white
light doesn't detract from the lesson.

Material you and the students create is best because it fits your lesson exactly.

*How Does the Overhead Projector Work
in Teaching Art Lessons?*

Presenting drawings, pictures and illustrations for lessons is easy. The overhead is helpful in motivating art lessons. When you are working with large groups the
projector enlarges the material so that it is easily seen. Small groups may sit close and
work with the machine drawing or moving objects for you.

Try the following lesson ideas using the overhead projector.

Drawing—Quick figure drawings, action drawing, line drawing, contour
drawings, calligraphy, etc.

Shapes—Shapes project dramatically. Have shapes precut from scrap paper
or cardboard. "What is a shape? Can we use many kinds of shapes
together in a design?" Manipulate shapes to form a pleasing composition
before gluing any design. Moving shapes around on the overhead stage
shows how to change a design. Repetition of shapes and varying their
size make designs more interesting.

Positive and negative concepts can be developed beautifully using
real objects on the stage of the overhead projector. Try keys, scissors,
wheels, gears etc. Find the negative shapes. Stress that the negative
area is as important as the positive area.

Show how to use positive and negative areas in a design using cut
paper shapes.

Color–How are colors created? Mount red, yellow and blue cellophane in
overhead frames. Use these as color overlays to show how secondary

colors are formed. Allow portions of all three colors to overlap each other and demonstrate how brown is created. Use shapes of colored cellophane to illustrate the overlapping of colors. A glass dish of water can be set on the overhead stage. Drop red, yellow and blue watercolor paint or ink into the water. What happens as they mix? Does this happen on paper?

Murals—Children can draw their own pictures and project them on large paper on a wall to compose a mural or to make a large drawing. Don't have children copy drawings from books.

Music and Art—Have the children draw and color a transparency series and select music to work with the art. They can play or sing their own music or use records.

The Dry Mount Press

Any time you want to permanently preserve a picture, design, poster or other teaching aids use the dry mount press. Directions for your specific model are available from the manufacturer. Your state department of education may offer a workshop demonstrating dry mount equipment and procedure.

Filmstrip and Movie Projectors

The filmstrip and movie projectors are additional audiovisual aids to help motivate and develop art lessons. Always preview the filmstrip or movie. Remember to use only what is applicable to your lesson. The light in the machines can go on and off if there are pictures you do not wish to use or if the material is too lengthy. Use the projectors as part of the lesson. Show the film or filmstrip through. Then show it again, this time stop and discuss the parts that are most important. If your group is small, have them sit close and project the image on a smaller area.

Films and filmstrip subjects in art are unlimited. There are how-to-do-it materials, art appreciation series, and those that show how artists work.

Blank filmstrips are available so that children may scratch into the black surface and create their own drawings for a series. Norman McLaren uses this exciting idea with musical backgrounds in his McLaren Films.

Slides—Children can create their own slides if they have scraps of acetate film or colorless Con-Tact paper and purchased cardboard mounting frames for slides. Colored slides are made using colored markers and transparent colored paper on the acetate sheet. Use scratch-out techniques with scissors or a compass point.

Make dimensional slides with two sheets of acetate. Place scraps of cellophane, tissue, colored threads, lace, loosely woven cloth, rickrack trim and so on between the sheets of film. If a slide gets too thick, some materials may be out of focus. Black-and-white slides are made by using India ink or black marking pens.

It is easy to photograph your own slides if you have an Ektograph. The Ektograph is a simple holder for an Instamatic camera and flashbulb. You can place two-dimensional illustrated material under the camera loaded with black and white or color slide film. The slides you make yourself are unobtainable elsewhere.

Have you ever thought how disappointing it was that a beautiful photograph or drawing in *Ideals* or *National Geographic*, or even in a fine art book, was too small to be seen by the class when you attempted to show it from the front of the room? Have you wanted to make a special collection using materials from many sources such as pamphlets, postcards, travel brochures, newspapers, calendars, library book illustrations or advertisements? Using an Ektograph, without cutting the source material out, a slide photograph is taken and can be developed first and then projected using a conventional slide projector. Sets of purchased slides can never be as exciting as a custom set. No photographic skill is needed to use an Ektograph. Everything is automatic. The school may have funds available to purchase one.

Movies—Some schools have movie cameras or a parent may allow children to use theirs. First have the children write or plan a sequence of events and then take the movie.

Records and Tapes—Have music played on record players or cassettes to set the mood for your art lesson. Keep a record or tape collection to use for this purpose. Your music teacher will help you select good quality recordings.

Video Tape Equipment—Video tape equipment consists of a television camera, a tape machine and a television receiver. Video tape records picture and sound so that it can be shown as the action takes place or at a later time. If you are lucky enough to have the equipment, you can tape your art demonstrations and use them again. A lesson can be presented in one area while it is shown on the television screen in another area. Original plays, children working, guest instructors and panel discussions are among the many other things you might record. A teacher can use the video tape machine to improve his or her own teaching techniques by seeing how he or she appears to others. Large industry has made use of video tape equipment in their training departments. Schools can often arrange to visit a local company for ideas by contacting the public relations or training department.

Use What You Have and Get What You Can

Books and Magazines

There is a significant difference between instructional art books published years ago and those off the press since the 1960s.

Replace the uninspiring, uniformly sized, textbook-type editions, which all have the same look and voluminous text. Select clear, colorful, well-illustrated material that attracts readers, whether the material is written for youngsters or adults. If your personal, class or school library has limitations or has not been updated, begin now.

Expensive volumes of paintings showing specific museum collections rarely leave the shelves. Avoid buying those and use your budget for inspiring books that present or discuss one type of art or one technique. Do not buy books that break down each idea leaving no place for imagination or adaptation.

If you expect the entire class to see an illustration that you hold up from the front of the room, make sure it is large enough. Twelve by fifteen inches is the minimum size for a book that will be used in this way. Try to see it from the back of the room yourself. One illustration on a page is all that can be seen clearly. Use an opaque projector for anything smaller.

Art magazines can also be excellent source material. Collect and cut out inspirational articles or illustrations that can be adapted to your needs. These magazines will be helpful. At least one article in each issue will be valuable to you.

Arts & Activities	Publishers Development Corp. 8150 North Central Park Avenue Skokie, Illinois
Ceramics Monthly	Professional Publications, Inc. 4175 North High Street Columbus, Ohio
Craft Horizons	American Craftsmen's Council 44 West 53 Street New York, New York 10019
Creative Crafts	Oxford Press 6015 Santa Monica Blvd. Los Angeles, California
Decorating & Crafts Ideas	P. O. Box 2327 Fort Worth, Texas 76101
Design Quarterly	Wacker Art Center Minneapolis, Minnesota
McCall's Needlework	McCall Pattern Co. 230 Park Avenue New York, New York 10017

Use What You Have and Get What You Can

School Arts

The Davis Press
Worcester, Massachusetts

Include as many of the following books as you can in your library. An asterisk designates that it is one in a series of valuable books.

Classroom Library

Title	Author	Publisher	Date
African Art	Dennis Duerden	The Color Library of Art	1971
African Crafts	Jane Kerina	The Lion Press	1970
Approaches to Drawing	Leo Walmsley	Van Nostrand Reinhold	1972
Art Appreciation— Enjoying the World of Art	Belves and Mathey	The Lion Press	1966
Art for Children	Jane Cooper Bland	Childcraft	1972
*The Art of the North American Indian	Shirley Glubok	Harper & Row	1964
Ben Shahn–Graphic Art	James Soby	Braziller	1963
*Claude Monet	Yvon Taillandier	Crown	1967
*Drawings of the Masters	Johnson, Hillier and Sérullaz	Shorewood Publishing	1964
How Artists Work	Belves and Mathey	The Lion Press	1968
Kathe Kollwitz Drawings	Herbert Bittner	Sagamore Press	1970
*Klee	Robert Fisher	Tudor	1966
The Many Ways of Seeing	Janet G. Moore	World	1970
*Marc Chagall	Ernest Raboff	Doubleday	1968
Picasso's World of Children	Helen Kay	Doubleday	

Resource Books

Title	Author	Publisher	Date
Batik, Art and Craft	Randall and Haines	Davis	1964
Bulletin Boards and Displays	Randall and Haines	Davis	1961
Collage and Construction	Harvey Weiss	Young Scott	1970
Collect, Print and Paint from Nature	John Hawkinson	Whitman	1963
Crafts for Children		Sunset	1973
Creating with Colored Paper	Lothar Kampmann	Van Nostrand Reinhold	1967
Creating with Paint	Seidelman and Mintonye	Crowell-Collier	1967

194

Use What You Have and Get What You Can

Creating Paper Craft	Chester J. Alkema	Sterling	1967
Creative Stitchery	Meilach and Snow	Reilly & Lee	1970
Making Contemporary Rugs and Wall Hangings	Donna Meilach	Abelard & Schumann	1970
Murals for Schools	Arne W. Randall	Davis	1968
Notan–The Dark-Light Principle of Design	Bothwell and Frey	Reinhold	1968
Off Loom Weaving	Marion H. Bernstein	Little Craft	1971
Paint All Kinds of Pictures	Arnold Spilka	Walck	1963
*Painting, I, II, III	Everett E. Saunders	Whitman	1968
Painting, Activities, Techniques, Materials	Virginia G. Timmons	Davis	1968
Pencil, Pen and Brush	Harvey Weiss	Young Scott	1961
Poster Ideas and Bulletin Board Techniques	Kate Coplan	Oceana Publications	1962
Step by Step Weaving	Nell Znamierowski	Golden Press	1967
Stitchery	Everett E. Saunders	Whitman	1966
Stitchery for Children	Jacqueline Enthoven	Reinhold	1968
Stitchery, Art and Craft	Nik Krevitsky	Reinhold	1966
Teaching Color and Form	Gottfried Tritten	Van Nostrand Reinhold	1971
Wall Hangings–Designing with Fabric and Thread	Sarita Rainey	Davis	1971
Weaving Without a Loom	Sarita Rainey	Davis	1966
Words and Calligraphy for Children	John Cataldo	Van Nostrand Reinhold	1967

Inspiration

Art as Image and Idea	Edmund Burke Feldman	Prentice-Hall, Inc.	1967
Art for Teachers of Children	Chandler Montgomery	Merrill	1968
Art Lessons on a Shoestring	Ruth Peck and Robert Aniello	Parker Publishing Co., Inc.	1968
Challenge Symbols to Encourage Children in Creative Expression	Mary J. Ellis	T.S. Denison & Co.	1957
Drawing, Ideas, Materials and Techniques	Gerald Brommer	Davis	1972
Emphasis Art	Wachowiak and Ramsay	International Text-book Co.	1965

A Handbook of Arts and Crafts	Wigg and Wankelman	Wm. C. Brown Co.	1961
The Many Ways of Seeing	Janet G. Moore	World	1968
Readings in Art Education	Eisner and Ecker	Blaidsdell	1966
What Can I Do for an Art Lesson?	Peck and Aniello	Parker Publishing Co.,Inc.	1972
With a Free Hand	Adelaide Sproul	Reinhold	1968
*The World of Leonardo, Michelangelo, etc.	Time-Life Library of Art	Time-Life	1966

Idea Books

One of the easiest ways to remember ideas you would like to try out or those you want to repeat is to make an idea book. A loose-leaf binder with plastic pages is perfect for inserting two-dimensional samples, magazine articles, lists, reminders or photographs. Magazines such as *Arts & Activities, School Arts, Family Circle, Design* (Quarterly), *Decorating & Craft Ideas, Sphere, Craft Horizons, Ceramics Monthly* and *Creative Crafts* all are excellent sources. Choose those articles that are adaptable for school use. Avoid gimmicky ideas stressing holiday time, patterns, or those that require purchasing expensive materials. Select art lessons that encourage creative thinking and use art skills. Try new ideas and those that use previously taught skills in a new way. No matter how well an article is written, don't forget to try the idea first.

Some lessons are not as successfully adapted to your particular needs as are others. Remember to teach the art skill first and use innovative ideas as a supplemental lesson another time once the skill is mastered. For instance, have the students explore the possibilities of various paintbrushes, thin ones, wide ones, easel brushes, and the soft camel hair type before you have a lesson on Japanese calligraphy.

Make your own idea books by organizing the collections of good photographs, graphic art, advertising layouts, famous paintings, new materials and other ideas you have saved.

Use a paper cutter and a dry mount machine to laminate the pictures on uniform-sized pieces of cardboard. Punch holes so that metal rings can be used to hold all the sections together in book form. Use Con-Tact paper on heavy cardboard as a cover.

Putting a collection in order is an involved job. An adult volunteer aide could easily work under your supervision.

Use these books in your class library and refer to them often.

14

Children
Have Opinions, Too!

Often you will find children voicing strong opinions about one another's work. They clearly state why they like or dislike a painting, drawing or design. How does a young artist take the criticism? How can we guide children to criticize constructively? When this situation arises, explain and then show the children that not everyone likes the same things. That is why there are so many kinds of ice cream. It does not mean that only one is good and all the rest are bad. The work of a well-known artist whose work is similar to the work of the children will allow everyone to talk about the art. Help the children realize that many people have strong opinions about famous works of art. Ask them if a picture helped the artist express something. Do they think the artist was always pleased with his work? Do artists realize that some things they do are not as well done as others? When their ideas and opinions are aired perhaps the group could discuss their own work more objectively.

What About Art Appreciation?

It is not always necessary to have formal art appreciation sessions. It is often better to let children look at art around them and talk about it. Always stress the arts and crafts of other cultures in social studies. Be sure to encourage visits to local art shows, exhibits in the school, public libraries, banks and museums. Check your art museum for a children's section. Before you visit a museum as a group, try to obtain the movie *Enjoying Art* (Perspective Films, 369 West Erie, Chicago, Illinois 60610). Have books, filmstrips and slides for children to use. Try to build a file of prints and reproductions of quality art work. Display these in the room. Do not expect children to relate to Rembrandt and the old masters without a solid art background. Start with more contemporary work that is more like theirs. Find pictures of art by Klee, Miro, Shahn, and the Impressionists. Keep these easy guidelines in mind as you encourage children to discuss art.

> Paintings and drawings are man's way to tell about himself.
> Let the child look and talk.
> Does the picture show . . .
> How the artist feels?
> His needs?
> Something he has seen or imagined?
> A way to show a new idea in a new way?
> How does an artist tell us these things?
> With color?
> Line?
> Form?

Color, line and form can be used in many ways.
   Realism
   Impressionism
   Abstraction
How did the artist use different ways to express himself?
Do you like the pictures? Why? Why not?

Three-dimensional work, sculptures, mobiles, statues and relief can be discussed in the same ways.

In addition, observe how the artist uses his materials to work in the round. Sculpture must be good to look at from every side and angle. Again encourage the children to express opinions about the work. Use the guidelines to help them state reasons for their opinions.

Most traditional art appreciation lessons include biographical material about the artist. This is often not important to children and the teacher must be sure of the accuracy of the facts about the artist before presenting them to the children. It is better to tell the children that Van Gogh loved the sun and its colors on fields and trees than to impress upon them that he was a mentally ill person.

When you are introducing a lesson, reproductions, slides or movies can be used to spark interest or present an idea, but put all this material out of sight when the children begin to work. Do not ask the children to copy Van Gogh's "Starry Night" or Degas' "Ballet Dancers" or any other painting. Instead let them paint or draw their own ideas of night or have children dance while others draw. Make it clear as you discuss artists and their work that each has an individual style and technique. A true artist does not imitate others but finds his own ways with the material as he creates.

There are several excellent series of fine art books for children (see chapter 13).

The Noncopyist

In your math, social studies or language arts lessons copying is definitely discouraged. Why is it permitted and advised in many art lessons? How many posters, book covers, school notices, P.T.A. bulletins and contest entries proudly display Snoopy or Charlie Brown, Mickey Mouse or other cartoon characters? Teachers are always praising the class cartoonist who is marvelously skilled in quick plagiarizing of copyrighted material.

Have the children ever been told that this is stealing? How can we channel the drawing ability of a child who is merely copying and not creating? Encourage each student to make up his or her own cartoon character and build a series of comic strips using them as the means to deliver ideas or messages. Have a lesson about how someone can secure a copyright to protect his ideas and help assure himself of a livelihood.

Children Have Opinions, Too!

Presenting one of the Warren Schloat filmstrips, "Hank Ketchum," creator of Dennis The Menace, is an excellent way to show the class how a cartoon character is developed. Mr. Ketchum tells how he started cartooning as a youngster and developed his own ideas.

Let the boys and girls go through newspapers, magazines and comic strips and find the ®, © or ™ marks that show that the idea is the property of someone else and that the owner's right is protected by law. Have a hunt around the room or have the children look at home to find and list copyright signs and trademarks. Share the finds by displaying the lists or making charts. Perhaps one or more children at this point would be interested in developing an idea and going through the actual process of securing a copyright. There are valid copyrights and patents held by very young children on toys, scientific tools and inventions. Don't underestimate your group.

Art Sensitivity in the Curriculum

Art is a part of life, not just a forty-minute class lesson on a Friday afternoon. Look for opportunities to show your students that in different cultures, Indian, Eskimo or African, for example, art is woven into the people's lives as a natural expression rather than a leisure-time activity or as an isolated profession. People in those cultures are not self-conscious about their art activities and do very little comparing of one person's artistic efforts to another's. To build art sensitivity in your curriculum minimize or eliminate giving grades for each piece of art work and emphasize your appreciation of effort, good attitude and creative use of art skills.

In many class discussions ideas come up that can be expanded to include weaving, murals, painting or drawing. Write a note to yourself to pursue these at another time. When an exciting idea evolves, scrap, postpone or change what you had planned. Let the class paint, draw or write about that fire engine that whizzed by the window. If the group is enthusiastic, or several children are, use that energy before it subsides. Encourage whoever is especially interested to work in his or her own free-time slots, after or before school or allow extra time for idea development. Have each one set a personal goal and a time limit. Permit the student enough time to finish, clean up and display the work. Don't put physical or time obstacles in his path. Encourage self-evaluation.

Fully develop an idea in all class disciplines. The same topic can be used in any grade by varying the level of sophistication. For example, boys and girls often learn about Paris in social studies. Firsthand information brings an enthusiastic response. School volunteer pools can often find someone who has lived in Paris or who is a native Frenchman to give the added impetus for a unit that involves everyone. The children can easily learn French words and phrases. Songs, films, slides and pictures are used to compare Paris with a city the children have already studied such as Chicago. The children draw pictures, learn to tie-dye and cut and glue the material on drawings they have made to design Paris fashions. Older groups can actually learn to use and create patterns and sew garments for dolls or themselves. The children learn that Paris has been known for its artists. Around 1800 a group, later named the Impressionists, studied and drew their inspiration from Paris and its environment. They painted outdoors and used light in their paintings. Students find out about Monet, Manet, Cezanne, Renoir, Van Gogh and other artists by hearing about them, seeing examples of their work and by learning to use watercolor, chalk and pen and ink techniques similar to those of the Impressionists. They can see a guest artist use oil paint and can smell it and apply it to the guest's canvas as they learn how to mix color and create different effects. Each day they learn about one of the artists and the technique he used. Observation is stressed when the children try to make a still life of their own. It isn't as easy as it looks. Sometimes music is played while they paint.

Library materials are available and the children are encouraged to make reports. In this way the boys and girls practice their cursive writing and language arts skills. A bulletin board and other displays are prepared including reports, printed illustrations and original paintings by the children. New vocabulary words are introduced and practiced. Differences in each artist's individual style are brought out so that when the class as a group visits the art museum with a guide, they recognize the paintings by the Impressionists and really begin to understand what the artists were trying to do. Back at school plans are made for a Parisian street market. Help is enlisted when necessary from the parents and teachers in making costumes, scenery, murals, vending stalls, canopies and signs. The children get fruit and cookies to sell, which gives them practice in basic math skills. Sidewalk artists draw portraits and exhibit their work. Music plays and French phrases are exchanged. It is the nearest thing to visiting Paris.

Many teachers, parents and students have art objects, books or collections gathered from trips or special interest areas that they can share with others. In the kindergarten and primary grades a scheduled show-and-tell activity is part of the curriculum. Older children have valuable ideas and things to display as well but rarely bring them to school without encouragement. The teacher should bring art items, books and articles to class for the students to look at. Ask the students to do the same. Many well-done programs on educational TV can be enjoyed by the group if they know about them in advance. Have a cultural arts committee who keeps the others informed through a special bulletin board or weekly newsletter, poster or ditto sheet.

How many lost opportunities there are when follow-up activities are ignored after a stimulating field trip, guest artist, special school program or news event has been experienced! What better motivation is there?

Become as sensitive to art in everyday life as you are to the individual needs of each student.

Index

Index

203

204

Index

Index